GROWING UP FEMINIST

GROWING UP FEMINIST

THE NEW GENERATION OF AUSTRALIAN WOMEN

Jocelynne A. Scutt

ANGUS
& ROBERTSON
PUBLISHERS

You do have to say ''no'' to
the old ways before you can begin to find
the new ''yes'' you need.

Betty Friedan,
''Epilogue'' in The Feminine Mystique, 1963

ANGUS & ROBERTSON PUBLISHERS

Unit 4, Eden Park, 31 Waterloo Road,
North Ryde, NSW, Australia 2113, and
16 Golden Square, London WIR 4BN,
United Kingdom

First published in Australia
by Angus & Robertson Publishers in 1985

Copyright © Jocelynne A. Scutt 1985

National Library of Australia
Cataloguing-in-publication data.
Scutt, Jocelynne A., 1947-
   Growing up feminist.
   ISBN 0 207 15139 3.
   1. Feminism — Australia.   2. Women — Australia —
   Social conditions.   I. Title.
305.4'2

Typeset in 10/12 pt Baskerville
Printed in Australia by
The Dominion Press — Hedges & Bell

Contents

Acknowledgements

I have received support in the writing and compilation of *Growing up feminist* from a number of people, in many ways. The ways include proficient and unstinting typing; provision of an office at a time it was welcome; discussion and debate on a number of issues relevant to discrimination against women and girls, particularly in education and medieval literature; suggestions for potential contributors, and sisterly support; and expert editing and publishing. The people include Jocelyn Terry, Carmel Niland, Frances Lovejoy, Pat Davies, Margaret Bradstock, Robin Joyce, Kerry Heubel and Felicity Beth, Rosemary Neilson and Richard Walsh. I thank them all.

Jocelynne A. Scutt
Melbourne, 1985

Introduction

Feminism is truly a venture into a terra incognita.

Rosemary Radford Ruether,
New Woman, New Earth, 1975

Why do some young women "grow up feminist"? Is it a result of family influences? schooling? role models? peer group pressures? or a rejection of each or any one of these? To women who have been in the women's movement for years, and who now sit about at Women's Electoral Lobby meetings, or Union of Australian Women meetings, Women's Liberation meetings and Women and Management, or Business and Professional Women meetings lamenting the lack of young women joining their ranks, these questions are crucial. Equally, for young women who are struggling in a world which does not universally accede to feminist ideals, yet who recognise the importance of equal rights for girls and women, the "why" of feminism is important.

It is important for young women and girls to have the opportunity to read what their peers believe in, and to recognise that they are not alone in believing girls are as good as boys; that cries of "yah, you're just a silly girl", or declarations that they are no good at maths are made without thought for female abilities and resourcefulness. Girls need to know they are not odd or peculiar because they believe in their rights and want those rights recognised.

This book is designed for young people — girls *and* boys — and adults. It is written to help young and old alike to understand both the historical origins of girls' and women's oppression and the present ideals and aspirations of young women who articulate feminist ideals. Present efforts to assist in the realisation of those ideals, and unmet needs which must be recognised if young women's rights to equality are to be attained, illustrate the difference between what we have now and what we must seek to gain for youth.

The contributors, ten young women between the ages of

sixteen and twenty-four years, come from a varying range of backgrounds. Mainly middle class in upbringing, their number includes girls who describe their families as working class. Some are of recent ethnic origin. Most are of Anglo-Australian descent. They were born in towns around Australia. Some have moved state between then and now. None is of Aboriginal descent, despite sincere efforts on my part to include black Australians. Perhaps this means that feminism is not as relevant to young women of Aboriginal descent, nor to young women born outside Australia who have emigrated here. The disadvantages they suffer through racial and ethnic intolerance by other Australians may be so great as to cloud the importance of sex-based discrimination and the problems it poses for them. Or it may be more appropriate that these young women speak their own vision of a recreated world in other volumes. The growing up of young Aboriginal women and young women recently arrived in Australia is equally deserving of forums.

A brief profile of each contributor is given below:

Anna Donald, after returning from France where she had been spending her school holidays in 1983, moved to Canberra from Sydney to complete her schooling. In 1985 she began studying medicine (combining arts and medicine) at Sydney University; in particular, she is studying physics, bodies and Italian. She says she is "getting educated to lead an interesting and challenging life as prescribed so flippantly by the school careers books and much less flippantly" by her mother. She is presently trying not to set any limits until she knows "more about life, the universe and everything — which at eighteen is pretty minimal".

Sarah Gillman graduated from the Canberra College of Advanced Education in 1984 with a Bachelor of Arts in Journalism. She began work at the Macquarie Network's Canberra radio station, 2CA, as a production assistant, and in March 1985 was promoted to the post of Grade 4 cadet journalist. She sees her career as being in the news and current affairs field and is saving for a trip to the Middle East.

Emel Corley, after completing her apprenticeship in motor mechanics in Brisbane in 1985, became involved in a women's circus project "for light relief". She also contributed to a CYSS project production of a tape about women in non-traditional work areas; the tape is to be used in schools. Emel says that she feels "very satisfied" with her achievement in motor mechanics, but feels "some trepidation at facing the job market as a woman mechanic, if and when" she leaves the circus. She is continuing to seek resources and support to enable a mechanical workshop run by women to be set up in the future.

Cathy Henry, after graduating in law from the University of New South Wales at the end of 1983, worked as a research assistant on the Satellite Inquiry at the Australian Broadcasting Tribunal. After her admission as a solicitor, she worked briefly on a number of policy/legislative projects for the Tribunal, and in 1985 took up a position as a legal officer with the New South Wales Legal Services Commission in Sydney.

Michele Trewick, graduating with a Bachelor of Arts from the Darling Downs College of Advanced Education in Queensland in 1984, completed her final exam at 5 p.m. on Wednesday afternoon and began holiday work at the *Queensland Times* at 9 a.m. the following day. That led to a full-time job with the *Times* as a fourth-year cadet and later a D grade journalist. She was sent to Los Angeles at very short notice to cover the release from hospital of Australian liver transplant baby Paul McKee, and in taking on that job was, she believes. "probably one of the youngest journos to be sent overseas".

Karen Ermacora completed her Bachelor of Arts degree in Dance (Performance) in 1984. Throughout that year she lived in an independent household with three others in Prahran, Victoria. In February 1985 she commenced work with the Tasmanian Dance Company as a full-time dancer, stationed in Launceston.

Mary Gartrell participated in the making of an ABC television documentary on sex education in 1983 and in 1984 completed the Higher School Certificate, having been a school prefect and member of the hockey team at North Sydney Girls' High School. Until beginning computer science studies at university, she worked part-time at babysitting and gardening. She is planning to return to Germany, where she lived as an exchange student, to study and work when she completes university.

Diana Forward began the third year of her Bachelor of Arts degree in Italian (Pure Honours) in 1985. When she finishes her course she intends to live in Europe for some years. One of her ambitions is to "work on getting the sexist elements removed from languages like Italian". She believes this to be "most likely an impossibility, but worth a try".

Jennifer Stott moved from her journalist's job with a glossy women's magazine in Sydney in 1984, combining her two major concerns and interests — women and film — to become the women's film worker at the Sydney Filmmakers' Co-op. In that position she promotes many of the films which she found significant upon first seeing them some years ago. With the passage of time, Jennifer Stott says, her "commitment and approach to feminism has opened up considerably, and through that broadening has become stronger".

Fiona Giles graduated from the University of Melbourne with a Master of Arts degree in English literature in 1985. She took up a tutorship in the Centre for Research into Australian Literature at the University of Melbourne, and was awarded a Commonwealth Scholarship and Research Plan Award tenable in the United Kingdom. Simultaneously, Fiona won the national Caltex Woman Graduate Prize for 1984, and intends to use the award to study overseas in 1986.

CHAPTER ONE

Education

[Mary Astell's seventeenth century proposal for women's and girls' education failed], though a lady of fortune, impressed by [Astell's A Serious Proposal to the Ladies], proposed to contribute 10,000 pounds towards erecting a seminary or college, for the education of young women . . . The execution of this laudable and rational project was prevented by Bishop Burnett, from a puerile apprehension, that its resemblance to conventual institutions would reflect scandal on the Reformation.

Mary Hays,
Female Biography,
or Memoirs of Illustrious and
Celebrated Women of all Ages and Countries,
Alphabetically Arranged, 1803

No one has better expressed the essential difference between the education of men and women than Mr John Burns in a speech delivered . . . at the North Surrey District School . . . Addressing the boys the President of the Local Government Board said, "I want you to be happy craftsmen, because you are trained to be healthy men." Addressing the girls he . . . used the following words:

"To keep house, cook, nurse and delight in making others happy is your mission, duty and livelihood."

The boys are to be happy themselves; the girls are to make others happy. No doubt Mr Burns spoke sincerely; but is he not one of the "others"?

Cicely Hamilton,
Marriage as Trade, 1909

In school books, the Dick and Jane syndrome reinforced our emerging attitudes. The arithmetic books posed appropriate conundrums: "Ann has three pies . . . Dan has three rockets . . ." We read the nuances between the lines: Ann keeps her eye on the oven; Dan sets his sights on the moon . . .

Letty Cottin Pogrebin,
"Down with Sexist Upbringing"
in The First Ms. Reader,
Francine Klagsbrun, editor, 1972

Outside home and family life, school plays the most important role in developing children's attitudes and aspirations. For
young women growing up in the 1960s, 70s and early 80s, was
the Australian school system designed to promote ideals of
equal rights for women and men, equal opportunities and
equal access for girls and boys to information, learning, career
expectations? Does it have a potential for developing strong
feminist beliefs in young women, notions of their value as equal
human beings, as valid as their male confreres?

For girls, the operation of the educational system from its
beginnings influences its present consequences. In Australia
the idea that everyone, from whatever class (social or
economic) or background, had a right to an education
developed early. The country's convict origins forced
authorities to accept that children should be educated out of
the "bad ways" of their errant parents. To prove that the
colonies were not wholly made up of "the criminal type", it
behoved them to ensure that from an early age children were
well versed in elementary education at least. Education would
give them a real opportunity for a life above the criminal lower
reaches of colonial society.

Between 1872 and 1895 all Australian colonies established
public primary educational institutions. This egalitarian
approach differed from the British. In England, according to a
study of colonial education in Australia, "conservative opinion
. . . agreed wholeheartedly with the Bishop of London's
conviction that it was 'safest for both the Government and the
religion of the country to let the lower classes remain in that
state of ignorance in which nature originally placed them
. . .' "[1] Yet, despite the language of equality in Australia, the
teaching of boys and girls was not without distinction on
grounds of sex. Discrimination against female students was
overt, both at primary level and above. For the youngest, girls'
schooling and boys' schooling took different paths: girls were
taught reading and writing, but not arithmetic. Sewing and
needlework instruction were regarded as essential for girls. In
the upper levels, the few secondary schools catered in the main
for boys. Where girls' secondary schools were built, they mostly
concentrated on "feminine arts", Paige Porter writes in
Women, Social Welfare and the State.[2] With tertiary education, from 1851 to 1882 the University of Sydney in effect

refused admission to women, and from 1854 to 1881 the University of Melbourne similarly kept them out. Women were not admitted to matriculation until 1881 and 1882 respectively in Victoria and New South Wales. Without matriculation, no one could study at university, unless a special dispensation was granted. Special dispensation might be given to boys from wealthy families which were able to manipulate the system, but girls were never "special cases".

Strong opposition was voiced to women entering university. Even men who were sympathetic to women's claims failed to recognise them fully. In 1879 William Manning, Chancellor of the University of Sydney, took up the issue in his second annual address, saying:

> My attention has been called to the question of admitting educated young women to the University Lectures in the branches of Physical Science — such as Chemistry, Botany, Vegetable Physiology, Mineralogy, and Geology .... The studies in question might undoubtedly be taken up with much advantage by young women ambitious of superior culture ...[3]

Despite his words, it was clear that women's education remained for him a low priority:

> I think ... that it will be better to let the question stand over till our School of Science has been enlarged ... The best course to be taken by the advocates of advanced education for women, would be to found some sort of affiliated college for them in the vicinity of the University. This, as we know, has already been done at Cambridge and Oxford ... The suggested College would come within the spirit, though probably not within the letter, of our Affiliated Colleges Act ... There should be no difficulty in adopting some temporary arrangements to commence with, if there really be a widespread wish on the part of young women and their friends for higher education under or "within" the University ...[4]

Thus, there was a difference in the treatment of women's right to be educated and that of men: despite the establishment of universities and colleges with moneys from general revenue and gifts and grants, women were not to gain *equal* access, but had to set about the difficult task of obtaining funds in order to duplicate what were treated as facilities for men. Not only would women have to raise money; women had additional burdens: most people continued to see them as having no right to a tertiary education. Atop this challenge, women had to contend with the suggestion that they were somehow not fully legitimate — "probably not within the letter" of the Act — and their position was on sufferance, the subject of "some temporary arrangements".

Even when women won the right to enter university as fully fledged students, anti-women attitudes persisted. Women were terrorised by efforts to exclude them from some faculties. When Ada E. Evans enrolled in Sydney University Law School, she began her studies in the absence of the Dean, Professor Pitt Cobbitt, whose place had been taken temporarily by Professor Jethro Brown. Professor Brown was amenable to a woman entering law school, but on his return from sabbatical leave Professor Cobbitt was reported to have demanded to know: "Who is this woman?":

> There followed a series of doors slamming, chairs banging on floors and bells ringing. Professor Pitt Cobbitt summoned Miss Evans to his presence and attempted to dissuade her from continuing her course, pointing out in his own crisp manner that she did not have the physique and suggesting Medicine as more suitable.[5]

Ada Evans persisted, but no doubt other women would not have reached the point of enrolling, or might have dropped out had they enrolled, due to the sexism inherent in the system and the sexist attitudes expressed by professors, lecturers and instructors.

The philosophy finding voice in universities was no less than an extension of attitudes existing in the schools. That girls attended school with less overt opposition does not mean discriminatory attitudes did not prevail. It does not detract from discrimination in fact — sums of money spent on girls' education were less than those spent on boys'; grants for sporting and science facilities were less for girls' schools than boys' schools; at coeducational schools, girls were allotted less spacious sectors of the sports and playgrounds, confined to domestic science classrooms, and refused entry to chemistry and physics laboratories.

Discrimination in schooling in the 1960s and 70s

Throughout the 1960s and 70s overt and covert sexism continued in both public and private schools. The problem of discrimination in an education system that today is billed as free, equal and conveying equal opportunities exists at all levels. Studies into classroom interaction between teachers and students in mixed classes[6] show that:

- boys get more attention from teachers than do girls
- boys are more often asked questions than are girls, despite girls waving their hands and indicating a willingness to participate
- praise and encouragement are more often directed at boys than at girls
- boys make more demands of teachers' time than do girls
- teachers are more concerned about "how the boys are doing" than "how the girls are doing"
- teachers know their boy pupils by name, know their characteristics, their foibles, their talents, strengths and weaknesses — even if the boys are classed as naughty or if they are relatively quiet, with little obvious personality
- teachers see girls in the classroom as an amorphous mass, without individuality, personality, talents or strengths; they are viewed as boring, uninteresting, passive, dull, submissive, without ideas or initiative
- if girls misbehave like the boys, they are more likely to be punished, and punished more severely for lesser "out of line" activities than are boys
- boys take up more space in classrooms and in general school areas such as the sports ground, playground and lunch shed
- teachers prefer to teach boys (whether the teachers are male or female)
- boys are seen as more capable than girls, and are asked to take on more complicated activities, more intellectually demanding tasks, and so on. Girls who ask questions about mathematics or sciences are often met with answers such as "it doesn't matter, don't you worry about it Nellie, you won't have to deal with it when you grow up . . ."
- where girls gain the attention of a teacher, it is likely to be

as a sex object, not as a thinking, intelligent human being with a desire for learning

- girls are classed as silly when they speak up, try to gain the teacher's attention, or simply want to join in the learning process; they are classed as (almost) "inanimate objects" when they remain silent — and therefore, whatever approach they adopt, are unlikely to receive praise and positive attention from the person who is supposed to be teaching them
- teachers think boys are brighter, have more potential, need to be drawn out; they think girls are "dumb", have little potential, are "goody goodies" if they perform well, and "hopeless" if they perform badly
- if girls are neat in their work, it is because they pay too much attention to detail, to trivialities, and do not pay sufficient attention to depth of a subject; if boys are neat in their work, this is a positive attribute, showing how skilled they are, how talented, and how capable of presenting an in depth argument in an impeccable manner
- if girls are untidy in their work, it is because they lack discipline, lack interest in their work, have their minds on other things — for example, boys, make-up, pop groups, movies; if boys are untidy in their work, this is often attributed to their creativity, their innovative minds, their urge to get things done with a minimum of fuss

The general result of this treatment by teachers is that most girls are confirmed in their belief (nurtured at all stages of their lives, sometimes by parental attitudes and actions, often by media images, by many teachers, and by the world in general) that they are not worth as much as boys, that their ideas don't count, and that they don't count.

For girls who grow up espousing feminist ideals, sexism looms large. Emel Corley, a student in Brisbane, describes school as "horrific". Karen Ermacora found school in a Perth suburb limited her horizons; it was necessary to leave to gain a broader perspective. Sarah Gillman notes that her female friends suppressed themselves, worrying about what others would think — and particularly, what the boys would think. Fiona Giles' school contemporaries valued physical achievement and moral conformity over originality, intelligence and affection. When Anna Donald tried unsuccessfully to describe sexism to her teacher, he laughed at her so that she felt stupid and somehow ashamed.

Not only are girls affected by discriminatory treatment and led to believe they are unworthy, boys are affected too — and they are confirmed in their belief that girls are worthless. Boys learn quickly that they are the only ones who matter, that they are all-important. Carolyn Ingvarson and Anne Jones' Australian research confirms this, drawing a parallel to the situation in Britain:

> When students at the equivalent of HSC level in the United Kingdom were asked about their own abilities, they used the number of interactions with the teacher to estimate their abilities and worth. Despite getting good marks, the girls do not see these as reliable as a standard to judge their value and ability, as [they do] the discussion with the teacher.
>
> Quote: "Rob says a lot, and Julian and Paul and Johnny too. They all make a lot of noise, all those boys. That's why I think they're more intelligent than us."
>
> Boys' perceptions are affected by this interaction . . . in that they believed that they were more intelligent than the girls. They were not aware of the marks which the girls were getting for their assignments, and had based their judgments on performance in class, seeing teacher attention as the most important criterion. Teachers were surprised and shocked that the girls were under-valuing themselves to such an extent.[7]

Despite the obviously negative effect classroom interaction with teachers (or lack of it) has upon girls, and the equally obvious negative effect that the downgrading of girls has on boys, some educationalists attempt to justify differences in teacher attitudes and the education system generally towards girls and boys. Some say girls in primary school do better than boys so boys need more attention or that teacher attitudes have more influence on boys than upon girls, particularly as to whether they like certain subjects, and therefore teachers should pay more attention to boys. It is suggested that girls can "just get on with it" without help, and thus help should be directed to where it is most required — toward the boys.[8] This runs counter to the argument, equally often voiced, that girls show little initiative, and probably means that girls are less likely to make trouble, so they can be ignored by teachers, whereas boys are noisy, troublesome and demanding. An equally strong argument is that the process should be reversed: girls should be paid more attention and given more praise than boys, to offset the unsympathetic messages girls receive from society outside the classroom.

As importantly, early childhood experiences of girls and boys influence their attitudes toward achievement and success in adulthood.[9] Because girls are generally nurtured from babyhood into greater dependence, are often encouraged not to think for themselves, and are socialised into placing great reliance upon adult and male peer approval (at least at high school level), their ability to achieve in the same way as boys, or their desire to achieve, has to overcome considerable barriers. It could be argued that teachers should acknowledge these early childhood influences, not by encouraging more dependence, but by giving approval and support to fortify girls. This would build girls up to a position where they could achieve more easily and gain satisfaction in their achievements, without as great a reliance upon external factors when they are older. It could help in overcoming apprehension girls might feel about gaining success. Girls' competence should be reinforced. In secondary school, where girls' performance rates drop markedly, teachers should be required to concentrate more upon their female students, and less upon the boys. But research has found that even teachers who are intent upon dividing their attention equally between boys and girls acknowledge that more than sixty to seventy per cent of their time is spent dealing with the male pupils.[10]

Certainly support, appreciation and attention from teachers are factors influencing the attitudes and esteem of girls. Anna Donald, living in Sydney, found high school more to her liking than primary school. At primary school she had little to gain from teachers or fellow students. At high school, many of the women teachers discussed women's achievements and the need to overcome stereotyped views of the female role. Sarah Gillman, finding herself out of step with most students when she wished to continue studying maths and commerce, transferred schools. The support of her new teachers, and particularly the role model provided by the school principal, were crucial developing her appreciation for her own achievements and those of other women. Mary Gartrell and

Diana Forward profited from the good advice of careers' advisers and specialist teachers who encouraged them to seriously consider entering non-traditional professional fields. Yet, obviously, standards throughout the school system remain variable. Fiona Giles found little support forthcoming from the school she attended in Western Australia, and Michele Trewick, at school in Queensland, was advised about conventional careers for girls. Fortunately, both were able to gain support elsewhere.

The single-sex-versus-coeducational-school debate

One suggested means of dealing with problems girls face in being taught in a sexist system is sending girls to single sex schools. The argument runs that girls will not be available as a negative reference group for boys (which seems to assist boys in achieving dominance and motivates them to achieve in "masculine" ways, in turn disadvantaging girls in the classroom and adulthood). Girls will not, therefore, suffer continual blows to their ego and esteem throughout their school days. Confirming this, Sarah Gillman and Anna Donald found their abilities were better appreciated and enabled to develop when they transferred from co-ed schools to all-girls' schools.

Research shows that girls studying at coeducational schools spend a large amount of time seeking the approval of boys in the classroom and playground, and too little time on schoolwork. Sarah Gillman found that her friends, who had while at primary school wanted to become astronauts and judges, hastily decided to become air hostesses and secretaries upon reaching high school. Studies indicate that the influence of boys in close proximity dramatically affects girls' work performance. As well, girls attending single sex schools participate at a higher rate in maths and science classes than do girls attending coeducational schools, and they achieve a higher standard of performance. Girls in coeducational schools are more likely to choose traditionally female subjects than are girls attending single sex schools. Simultaneously, boys at coeducational schools are more likely to choose traditionally male subjects.[11]

However, genuine difficulties inhibit proposals that single sex schools should be set up for girls, or that all girls should be

enrolled in those already existing to overcome the discrimination inherent in the present coeducational system.
Paramount is the problem of forcing educational authorities to
recognise that coeducation is bad for girls. As Dale Spender
points out in her book, *Invisible Women — The Schooling
Scandal*, since coeducation was first introduced into Britain at
the end of the nineteenth century, protests have been voiced by
women about its harmful effects on girls. These protests have
been ignored, because coeducation is viewed as beneficial for
boys: with coeducation they always have a reference group they
can feel "better than".[12] And even if authorities recognised the
debilitating effects of coeducation on girls, could the
coeducational programme be reversed, with the education
dollar redirected toward the establishment or perpetuation of
single sex schools? It is unrealistic to suggest that increasing
single sex schools is likely to be a federal or state government
initiative. Even more importantly, if moneys were directed to
single sex schools only, even with the present government's
policies of equality of opportunity, how to ensure that moneys
are divided equally between boys' and girls' schools? Past
experience shows too clearly that the "separate but equal"
doctrine holds out little hope for equality in the sharing of
funds, facilities and other essential (and less essential)
resources. Finally, would single sex schools really overcome the
problem of denigration of women and the putting down of
girls' achievements? Would girls emerge from single sex schools
with feminist opinions and lifestyles, and with the ability to
sustain these in the world outside? And would boys learn of
women's achievements and equal rights, and abjure sexism?

   The problem of girls' schooling lies not only with male
teachers and coeducation. Dorothy Smith writes in *Women's
Studies International Quarterly*:

> Though women's participation in the education process at
> all levels has increased in this century, this participation
> remains within marked boundaries. Among the most
> important of these boundaries . . . is that which reserves to
> men control of the policy and decision-making apparatus of
> the educational system.[13]

Commenting on this, Dale Spender points out:

> Men have decided what education will be and women who
> seek only equal entry to that system simply seek equal rights

to the education of men which is designed to serve men. For women, equality will consist of equal *control* of education, and this is a very different matter indeed.

Because men got there first, they held all the powerful positions. They decided what would be taught, how it would be taught, and to whom it would be taught on the basis of the limited evidence that was available to them from their male experience. And while over the last centuries there have been some modifications in their ideas about who should be taught, and education was extended from the male upper and middle classes to encompass the working class, and blacks, and women of all classes and cultures, there has been little or no reduction in the control of what will be taught, nor how it will be taught. Because of this, women's gains have been minimal.

Where some (few) women have entered the power structure, they have been required to depend on male approval and support for their positions, and this has been one of the reasons that they have frequently "toed the male line" rather than try to develop their own. Because of this, women, even in positions of power, "do not ordinarily represent women's perspectives" . . . for "They are those who have been passed through this very rigorous filter. They are those whose work and style of work and conduct have met the approval of judges who are largely men. And in any case, they are very few."

Men have set up the system and they control it. Such control can be used to appoint to their ranks only those who will help to *perpetuate* male control of *what* is taught and *how* it is taught. [This control does not use such] obvious [tactics] as advertisements for candidates who profess staunch allegiance to the principle of male dominance, of course, but [there are] many means whereby "the best candidates" for influential positions appear to be males, or females who are indebted to males . . . [14]

Vital to the debate about single sex education being right for girls and women, or the only sound way to ensure girls grow up with a positive image of themselves, is that women would *not* control the course of girls' education, and those with a modicum of influence would not necessarily be women-centred women. With schools run by the state, curriculum control would, as now, be exercised by a male-dominated hierarchy.

With private schools, control over what is taught — at least in relation to core subjects, and by external means, in the setting of standards for entry to university and other tertiary institutions, as well as to trade and professions — would be dictated, in the main, by men.

With the passage of sex discrimination legislation at federal level, an effort is being made to develop a less discriminatory educational milieu. Such legislation recognises girls' and women's right to equality, but the danger always remains that with men in control of all institutions, including the executive, the legislature, and the bureaucracy, patriarchal problems will continue to surface. As long as men remain in control of all powerful institutions, the enforcement of rules advantaging men and disadvantaging women and girls will be more likely than adherence to rules advantaging women and girls and disadvantaging — or acting neutrally upon — men and boys.[15]

But at least efforts are being made in the government school system to ensure that, as far as possible in a patriarchal world, equal opportunities for girls become philosophically and practically the norm. Private schools do not come within the terms of the *Sex Discrimination Act* 1984 (Cth), nor within those of equal opportunity and anti-discrimination legislation existing in other states. Church schools, single sex or otherwise, are not controlled by women, nor by those who accept that women's rights are equal with those of men. Rather, they adhere to traditional views of women as subservient to men, in accordance with religious teaching. This was clearly illustrated in 1984 in Victoria, where the principal of a denominational girls' school was removed by the school board, despite staunch support from "old girls" and parents of many current students. The board, dominated by men adhering to the traditional view of "woman's place", refused to tolerate a principal who had strong feminist teaching principles. The furore died. The board won. A male principal got the job. And even where no such overt assertion of male dominance occurs, male dominance is endemic. As Sarah Gillman points out, despite the important role models teachers provided at her all-girls' school and the latitude granted to pupils in researching women's achievements and social topics, male achievements are focused on in single sex schools as well as in coeducational schools. It is difficult to avoid this: textbooks, historical records and literature ensure it is so. A change in focus to women's achievements as primary, or even equal, is slow in coming.

And what of teachers in single sex schools? With the introduction of a segregated system, would all teachers in girls' schools be women? A problem for girls' schools in the past which remains today is that some subjects are not taught by women, or too few women teach them. Although more women teach sciences today than previously, insufficient women teachers exist in *all* traditionally male subjects — maths, sciences, woodwork, metalwork — as well as those subjects traditionally the concern of women, to fill all places in girls' schools. Even if it were possible to select women teachers in sufficient numbers for all subjects, women will not invariably be positive influences on girl pupils. Not all women teachers convey esteem and other positive attributes; they too can fall into the trap of denigrating women's qualities and the abilities of girl students. All-girls' schools have not been fountains of wisdom in education about women's achievements and potential. Many have been no more than finishing schools designed to "finish" any aspirations girls might have to achieve in their own right and to make them more amenable to the world in which they will take their place; the girls are trained to become superior hostesses for men who believe they have a right to dominate and should rightly be in charge of business and in control of the world — and women. Adopting a policy of single sex schools would not ensure this problem was overcome.

Teachers' colleges are dominated by men, as are the universities. It is here that women (and men) learn to be teachers. They are influenced by what they have directly and indirectly been taught. As Dale Spender says in her book, there are women who "fail to learn" — but are there enough, and will they all take up the teaching role?

There are women ... who remain unconvinced about the female lack of authority, who do not accept the justice of women's exclusion from the education system (or for that matter the justice of any of the other social arrangements) and who will not subscribe to the principle that, when all things are equal between the sexes, then it is more reason-able to choose a man. They will not repudiate their experi-ence as autonomous human beings, and insist on the value and validity of their lives. These are the women who cannot necessarily be relied upon to act in the male interest if appointed to influential jobs and it probably helps to explain why there are so few feminists in policy and decision making positions ... Such women are *difficult*.

There are numerous ways in which they can be perceived as unsuitable for holding influential positions in the system men have set up: there are many areas in which they can be perceived as wrong, or deficient. For example, in a society which assumes the politeness and deference of women towards men as the norm, women who do not defer to men are often judged by women and men as socially unacceptable. Women who try to assert the strength and independence of women (in a society in which men have not accorded women strength and independence) are bound to be labelled aggressive, which is not at all deferential, and there is no end of the number of jobs for which aggression in a female is a disqualification ... [16]

And what do we want girls (and boys) to learn at school in relation to achievement, worth, human relations and human striving? In *Youth—Expectations and Transitions*, Millicent Poole points out that boys learn they should get ahead by way of wealth and status. The school system, and the world outside, tell them that this is how they should achieve; this is how their successes should be measured. Girls on the other hand generally learn that self-realisation is important, conceived in broadly humanistic educational goals. [17] Other writings refer to the affiliative motives which persuade girls and women to choose particular paths for study, work, career and general living patterns. [18] Do we necessarily want to change that part of girls' and women's orientation? The danger in adopting the view that to overcome sexism toward schoolgirls single sex schools must be promoted is that girls may begin to pursue those goals boys and men set for themselves. Is the aim, then, to ensure that girls are taught to compete in the world as it exists, or is it to change the world, making it capable of accepting as of equal value a diversity of talents and achievements?

If people are happy with the goals men set for themselves and believe girls should be encouraged to pursue these same goals, in the same way as men, then girls should be enabled to develop similar motives as boys. Girls should be educated out of the affiliative motives and desires for self-realisation which have been inculcated in them. Yet if people want society to change so that *all* — boys and men, girls and women — seek and can find self-realisation, affiliation, and caring for others, it is important to promote a system in which cooperation rather than competition is the mode. It is questionable whether co-operation rather than competition is being taught in the single sex schools which are promoted as enhancing the lives of young women. In single sex schools, deprived of girls to denigrate, boys create a scapegoat class of boys who are seen as sissy, hopeless, the dunces of the class. This, as in coeducational schools, assists the dominant group to achieve. Predictably, girls run the same risk of creating a downtrodden class of "dumb" girls in single sex schools.

Changing schooling values

The federal Labor government has recognised the deprivation suffered by girls in the past and present education system. The government gave priority in the allocation of funds to "projects of national significance" in education, the 1984 grant including $250,000 earmarked for the education of girls. The Schools Commission was to report on the impact of all its programmes on the education of girls. Schools are recognised as being capable of doing "much to assist girls to gain the confidence and competence necessary for equal participation in today's society".[19] A special computer education programme was to be introduced with priority given to access by girls and disadvantaged groups.

To change schools so that they encourage all girls to re-cognise their worth, with a real opportunity to grow up feminist, it is necessary to look at additional ways funding can be used to overcome those factors which prevent equal educa-tion rights for girls. Funding should be spent on non-sexist training for teachers, alerting them to their own classroom activity and training them not to ignore the girls. Male as well as female teachers should be required to attend non-sexist training classes. All teaching in training colleges and universities must complement in-house courses to make pro-spective teachers aware of sexism and methods to combat it. Women-centred women should be promoted to inspectors' positions so that they have control over who become teachers and who are placed on promotion lists. In grading teachers, those with control over classifications should be required to take into account those attributes which are important for changing the educational system: teachers who spend equal amounts of time with girls as with boys should be more highly graded than those who cannot overcome their sexist conditioning. There must be incentives so that advantages for teachers who try to overcome sexism and make efforts to follow non-sexist practices in the classroom are built into the education system.

Women must be promoted in equal numbers with men, so they can gain equal control over curriculum development and general education policy. They must hold equal positions of authority within the schools and the administration.

At the same time, boys have to learn too that women and girls have a right to be treated as full human beings, of equal value as men and boys. Boys are taught by the present school system that they are better than girls. If they do not come into contact with girls in the classroom who *are* being treated equally as they are, who *are* being given equal attention, and whose contributions to classroom discussion *are* given equal credence, then they will not learn that girls are their equals. Boys' ideas about their own superiority will be perpetuated and strengthened, rather than challenged and changed. If girls are hived off into a separate system, boys will never be required to learn about women's rights, historically and practically, through interaction in the classroom. Similarly, male teachers will never learn unless they are confronted daily with the need to overcome their own sexist upbringing.

Women must not be sacrificed to men, nor girls to boys, in order that boys and men may become more appreciative human beings. In the classroom, teachers should draw to the attention of girls and boys the injustices occurring in their own milieu as well as in the world outside. The differences in treatment of girls and boys, women and men, should be the legitimate subject of comment. As Susan Cosgrove says:

> Since we have discussed the problem [of my paying more attention to the boys than the girls] in the classroom, the girls have reported that the boys tend to take over their experiments if they work with the boys and they are left to

record ... I had noticed this and I always encourage girls to work with girls in the laboratory ... When I reported my findings [about the boys' conduct, and about my concentrating on the boys] the girls said that they had noticed the small amount of time that I spend with them, but they were so used to it that they had learned to cope ... They assured me that I was not the only teacher who did this. They said that they *all* did! *The boys said they weren't aware of any of this. Since then we have kept a check on the amount of time I spend with the girls or boys. The girls are learning to be more assertive and ask for my attention, and the boys have been trying to curb their demands and are trying to cope with their problems before they ask for attention.*[20] [Emphasis added]

Simultaneously, to ensure that girls have back-up support and reinforcement for the development of self-esteem and appreciation of other girls' and women's abilities, single sex classes should be established within coeducational schools. In this way, girls will have a real opportunity to learn about solidarity amongst women and the value of developing strong friendships and networks with other women, whilst operating within a mirror mini-society in other, coeducational classes. Ingvarson and Jones suggest that this is important:

How does one begin to change [the negative] pattern? It is long established, and girls will not suddenly on instruction, become more prepared to discuss issues, nor boys take a back seat. Seeking out answers from girls in the whole group works for some girls, so try it; but it can be counter productive for others.

Asking the more shy girls to read aloud their written work, and then to answer questions from the group can be a helpful start. Small group discussions, with boys and girls in different groups, at least for part of the time, can help to ensure that everyone has an opportunity to speak. Reporting the discussion back to the class and taking questions can further extend their communication skills.[21]

Educationalists suggest that small group work amongst girls is particularly vital in some subject areas. With science and maths, subjects in which girls have traditionally been taught to ignore their abilities, single sex classes may be vital to the promotion of feelings of competence, leading in turn to greater proficiency. Lynne Symons refers to the need for "small group work for girls to have a 'hands on' approach to science, especially in the areas where the boys have previous knowledge", for example, in electronics.[22] Barbara Small and Judith Whyte, writing up their work on an action research project based on schoolgirl under-achievement, conclude that school-based efforts should be "initiated and supported . . . to improve girls' attitudes to physical science and craft subjects, and to encourage more girls to study these subjects when they become optional". They suggest it is important to implement girls-only clubs in science or technology, "where girls can gain confidence in handling tools away from any possible ridicule from the boys".[23] This method has tended to redress the imbalance where boys are advantaged not only by attitudes within schools, but also through their greater experience with "tinkering activities outside school".

If society is to change so that girls are not subjected to denigration (and later, as women, subjected to discrimination on an equally grand scale), schools must be created where cooperation is the key and where positive attitudes towards women are fostered. Equal treatment will not be possible unless women and men cooperate in creating such schools. Ultimately, the world will remain dedicated to acquisitive ideals which in themselves promote discrimination against certain groups, of which the major group is women, unless girls and boys are taught together that girls are not to be despised, and that girls' value and worth are equal to those of boys. Until that time, young women striving to live out the feminist ideal of equality will recall their schooldays with a pain that should not be there. Like Anna Donald, they may grow up to say:

> . . . most of my friends were boys. But then . . . I learned that that kind of attitude didn't get you very far. I learned that I was a girl.

Anna Donald

Anna Donald, *sixteen years of age when her piece was written, was attending North Sydney Girls' High School in New South Wales and had not yet decided what career she would follow.*

Sixteen, in between, and growing up a feminist. Where can you begin? Sixteen, supposedly an age of finding out who and what you are, when life is no longer nice and undeep and meaningful, yet you still have to learn about practically everything that will make you somehow "experienced". I don't really know much at all yet about where I'm heading, but I do know one thing: that I am a feminist, which to me means having the freedom to choose what I want out of life on the basis of being a person, not a female.

For me there was no magic moment when there was light and there was feminism; to show how and why I adopted feminism, when the chance came, I have to go back to primary school, growing up a kid and growing up a girl — and being and seeing for myself what that means . . .

When I was little, my dad won a law scholarship to Harvard, so we packed up our bags and went to live in America for two years. Students are never rich, and one way of economising was home-done haircuts, which thanks to Dad's pudding-basin technique and my bought-to-last trousers and skivvies meant that I was very often mistaken for a boy. I must have been very naive; in America I went to a school where candy pink ribbons were in, and my crew cut and boy's pants were definitely out, yet at the time I was quite oblivious to being different, like a small Eve before eating the apple. Even when every day several perfumed little Shirley Temples would come up to me and say: "Are you a girl or a boy? You're a boy. Yuk. We don't like boys", I never worried about it. Anyway, most of my friends were boys.

But then we came back to Australia, and I learned that that kind of attitude didn't get you very far. I learned that I was a girl. For the first time I went to school in a uniform. I hated my black tunic; it made my legs cold, and as my tights wouldn't stay up, Mum had to fix them to my undies with safety pins. My crew cut wouldn't grow back, and my American accent didn't help making friends any easier. But worse than the haircut, the accent and the bunched-up tights, was learning to play the games that somehow I had never caught onto in the States. Learning that kicking a ball to Rodney meant you loved him, and that boys played cricket while the girls watched and talked about what spunks they were. It was all wrong, and no matter how hard I tried, I never did learn the rules, and it was hell. It can only have been for a year or two, but it seemed like a lifetime that I didn't "fit in".

I learned the hard way that I was a girl, but never really understanding what this meant made me afraid and then hostile against anything that the image implied. Among other things, I flatly refused to wear pretty clothes, not because I didn't like them, but because I was afraid they would mark me as something that I didn't understand and could never be. I became pretty hostile towards boys, whom I felt were traitors. They'd been my friends in America, why wouldn't they be here? What did they want from me? If all they wanted was admiration, then they could forget it. Sitting on brick walls was no fun. It made me very awkward with them. So I was a girl. Why did it mean so much to everyone else and so little to me? I became very wary of doing anything that would draw attention to myself, took up reading and spent lunchtimes in the library.

In fifth grade I moved schools again; I was sent to an "OC"

class where everyone was new, so for once I wasn't the only one who didn't know where the loo was. I wasn't exactly a roaring playground celebrity there, either, but as that class was full of kids who weren't too sure of themselves, no one looked at you and you stopped feeling so different. Also, I guess I was more or less Australian again by that time.

One day we learnt Strauss's "Wine, Women and Song" on our recorders, and I proudly took the music home to show Dad how difficult it was. To my disappointment, he didn't even look at the notes, but said: "What a sexist Strauss must have been." I asked him what that meant and he told me that (it meant that) as far as Strauss was concerned, women were only good for pleasure, like wine and song. I couldn't really see what was wrong with pleasure, but I scrawled SEXIST across my music anyway; Dad always knew what he was talking about. The next day I came in from lunch to find a crowd of boys giggling over my music, and realising that all they could see in the word was "sex", I felt vaguely embarrassed. Then my teacher came in, and laughing, asked me what it meant. Not having understood Dad's explanation, I couldn't tell him. He laughed harder, and I felt stupid and somehow ashamed, and soon forgot about it. In sixth grade I got involved in producing a school magazine, and worries about boys and differences disappeared in lunchtime printing sessions and piles of kids' poetry. I also made a best friend who wasn't too popular either, and together we forgot boys who didn't seem to care about anything but handball, and couldn't even write poetry.

Boys can't have meant very much, because when the next year we both went to North Sydney Girls' High School (one of the few remaining segregated state high schools), neither of us noticed the difference. But we changed a lot that first year of high school. It was that year that Mum started writing pamphlets for the Anti-Discrimination Board, the Women's Coordination Unit and the Women's Advisory Council, as well as giving lectures on sexism in children's literature. Suddenly the dining room table was covered with Fay Weldon and Miles Franklin, and spurred on by her course, Mum bought me a biography of Emily Pankhurst. I loved biographies, so I quickly finished that, learning a whole new list of words like "suffragette" and "feminism" (which up until then I had always confused with "feminine"). For my birthday I got books like the writings of Margaret Mead and *Other Choices for Becoming a Woman*.

Although I'd been told about sex for as long as I could
remember, Mum and Dad thought it was time I learned some
details, and gave me that marvellous Boston women's book
(with the green cover). They needn't have bothered; I'd
already read most of it, my curiosity aroused from kids at
school sneaking it behind the heater in the library and giggling
over condoms all lunchtime. Dad, the model modern father,
was terrified that I might be afraid to ask questions (having
been left in the dark by his parents), and tried to make me talk
"freely and openly about sex", like all the child-raising guides
recommended. He was disappointed; I wasn't particularly
fascinated by any of it, even the thought that Mum and Dad
"did it", and that no doubt so would I, one day. At twelve, boys
were a write-off, and I wasn't going to think about them until
they became more interesting to talk to.

But the feminist books interested me. Emily Pankhurst
became a hero, inspiring me to find out all I could about feminism. In social science we logically enough had to give a talk on
something social, so I chose to talk to the class about feminism.
They were most impressed with my tales of Chinese women's
snapped arches and women's struggle for the right to vote. I
gained a reputation as a radical feminist, not in a nasty way at
all, although I doubt that in year seven anyone, including me,
really knew what it was all about. I was suddenly very glad to
be born a girl: how boring it must be, I thought, to be born a
boy with nothing to fight for. At North Sydney I had an
audience and I had friends. Gone were the days of feeling
horribly inadequate and despising this thing they called a
"girl".

Feminism gave me a cause: almost a philosophy, a way of
looking at things. It gave me confidence to be what I wanted; I
could be a girl in my own right and be proud of it. But I never
forgot what it was like to be rejected, which made feminism all
the more important, because I saw that that was what feminism was trying to combat: stereotyping and rejection, my two
prime enemies. I theorised that acceptance was a need, like
food and water, but even more important. Why else did Daddy
Warbucks adopt Little Orphan Annie? Being accepted for
what you are, not what the world brands you as, feeling free to
choose what you want, to make your own list of priorities
according to *your* needs, not constantly feeling obliged to cater

for everyone else's: that is what I came to see as women's rights
— or more precisely, *humans' rights*. Maybe one day feminism
can be called "peoplism", when the scales have balanced, and
there is no longer any need to accentuate the fact that women
are people.

When the scales balance: learning about heroes of the
1900s was one thing; learning about today's reality was quite
another, I soon found out that being a feminist is not easy.
Becoming aware of sexual inequality and exploitation in a
world where chocolate is sold by women's bums is a disillusion-
ing process. It means having a conscience which you cannot
and must not ignore, although it complicates things, like
relationships with boys.

In years eight and nine we started seeing more kids from
the boys' school, and to them feminism was something their
older sisters bored them with, and was at best a bit of a joke.
Stating that I was a feminist branded me just as much as any
other stereotype, automatically implying that I therefore
burned my bra, hated boys, and was no doubt a lesbian, and
definitely a bit of a weirdo. These assumptions formed a pretty
hard wall which I got tired of bashing my head against, and it
was only thanks to having good friends who stood up for me
that I never gave up altogether, although I don't hate boys, I
don't burn my bra, I'm not a lesbian, and everyone's a bit of a
weirdo in their own way, feminism or no feminism. I knew per-
fectly well that explaining how important it is, and why, for
instance, jokes about Marilyn Monroe aren't funny would not
only hit deaf ears but also make me pretty unpopular. Knowing when to object to something, and when it just wasn't worth
it took a lot of working out. I wanted so badly to show them
that I wasn't trying to be boring and hostile; that all I wanted
was for them to understand that girls need to be given a chance
to be people, and constant cracks about their legs weren't
going to do much for them. But how do you explain to boys
that the reason girls are lousy at catching cricket balls is
because for a start they've never had any practice, but more
importantly that they don't have any confidence — to those
who don't know what lack of that kind of confidence, anyway,
means? I guess one of the reasons that made me stick to feminism was just that: girls' lack of confidence in themselves, that
was so obvious at school. If you don't *think* you can do
something well, you can't. You don't need positive thinking

psychology books to tell you that if you start something assuming you'll fail, then your chances of failing are an awful lot higher than for someone of the same ability but with more confidence about succeeding. Try walking across a plank first a few centimetres, then two metres off the ground. Your chances of falling the second time are a lot greater, from fear. Girls have a lot of fear. Fear of trying the unknown, because the world tells them they won't make it, which does nothing for their image, or for the credibility of (sexual) equality.

From Mum, and my own experiences, I reckoned that sexism, like any other prejudice, is a result of ignorance and lack of understanding. The only real remedy is education. Education about how people feel — but it must be taught to both "sides" and involve more than learning about the birds and the bees. Do boys have any real idea of how girls feel behind the smiles and make-up? And vice versa. Yet how do you teach something like that?

At school our "Personal Development" programme started off on a wonderful note: "Hair Curling", which for those of us whose hair frizzed into knots all by itself seemed rather pointless. Evidently my mother wasn't the only one who had something to say about it, for after a few weeks they stopped the course, and we changed to a new topic: "Personality". This rather ambiguous subject which was supposedly to help you identify your personal strengths and weaknesses was nevertheless great fun, involving filling in lots of little boxes about what you liked and disliked. One of the discussion questions was marriage, and what did we think of it? That threw us a bit. We had all sort of assumed since the days of playing mummies and daddies that marriage was inevitable, but with over half the class with divorced parents, we could hardly take it as the eleventh commandment: "Thou shalt get Married." It became quite a topic for debate. In the end there were about four who definitely wanted to get married, a whole lot who were undecided, and even more who didn't want to get married at all, because "divorce was too much of a hassle". One thing seemed definite, and that was that everyone wanted to be able to live with a prospective husband for a long time before marriage.

I think being at a girls' school influenced us a lot, particularly as all our teaching was based on preparing us academically for a world in which we'll have to have a career, but not necessarily a husband. A lot of our mainly women teachers were feminist supporters, and the problem of sexual inequality and what it could mean for us was often raised in class. With the very high divorce rate, girls *are* a lot more wary about marriage. In class we thought that ideally marriage should be an arrangement of living with someone you love on an equal *emotional* basis, which involves compromising with each other's needs. I often wonder how many of us will get married, and on what basis. Boys still seem to want to.

With marriage arose the question of children, which again produced an interesting response. (I wonder what Mum and her friends would have said about it at fourteen.) With regards to feminism, I wanted to say that being a feminist doesn't mean refusing to be a parent, but *choosing* to be a parent because you want to, not because you are female and therefore somehow obliged to have children. I'm not a parent, but I should think that it is one of the most difficult jobs in the world, involving up to a lifetime of full-time service for which there are no rules, no holidays, and always the ultimate question to face up to: am I a good parent? It would also be one of the most rewarding jobs and one of the most heartbreaking, and I think it's crazy to undertake it if you don't really want to. As far as fathers' roles as parents are concerned, I know that having a father who was an adept nappy changer, lunch-maker, bedtime storyteller and shoulder to cry on (all of which he had to learn, like anyone else) influenced me in my firm belief that fathers can and must share parenthood; if they don't they are not only leaving an enormous load on the mother, but are also missing out on a lot. I remember hearing of a family whose mother had to prepare two weeks' worth of frozen meals to go on holiday, and being quite amazed, wondering if perhaps the father was very severely handicapped and so couldn't manage to cook up chops or something.

My beliefs in feminism as giving women the right to feel free to choose what they want out of life applied to my ideas about a career, another "Personal Development" topic. Again, in spite of the "women's libber" stereotype, feminism to me doesn't mean denouncing typically "female" professions. It just means being free to choose from others as well. At first I wanted a very "unfemale" career to prove to the world that, as I was female, such a thing doesn't exist, but now I know I'll try to choose what interests me. But at sixteen none of us really know much about what we want out of life, which brings me back to where I started — sixteen, in between — and it is, too, knowing there are decisions to be made, but not yet experienced enough to make them. Still, I know that when I do start deciding, I'll only have myself to blame if I don't choose correctly, because thanks to my belief in feminism I'll be choosing from options limited by my ability, not my sex. Fifty per cent of the world is female, but one hundred per cent is human, with lives to live to as full a capacity as possible, which means choosing from options as *people*.

Sarah Gillman

Sarah Gillman *lived in Queanbeyan, a New South Wales country town, at the time of writing. She was nineteen years old and studying journalism at the Canberra College of Advanced Education.*

As we progress further into the 80s, society's perception of feminism is becoming increasingly misguided. Feminists are all seen as overweight, overalled, spike-haired lesbians, while feminism itself is regarded as a radical movement concerned with separatist, "man-hating" politics. However, feminism is not a set of dress rules. Nor is it a script for an alternative lifestyle play. Feminism is not an image. It is a way of life, an attitude to living which pervades the lives of many women. Feminists are mothers in suburbs, women in factories, students. They are diverse, ranging from those women focused on by the media, the "marxist-lesbians", to company executives and ballerinas. As feminists, they are individuals and, more importantly, independent individuals. For feminism allows women to live free of any artificial restrictions which try to mould them into an entity others have created for them.

I have always been a feminist because I have always thought of myself, and been regarded by my family, as an individual.

There are few males in my family. I am the eldest of three daughters, my mother the eldest of four. Until I was ten or so, my father was home only spasmodically. A journalist, he worked in Vietnam, and then for politicians, and consequently I was not exposed to the sexist role-playing that usually occurs with the nuclear family. My mother undertook the tasks generally assumed by males and in my early years I was surrounded by strong, capable women. Even when my father resumed a more patterned home lifestyle, his literary mind refused to combat practical or mathematical problems and my mother continued to file the tax, paint the hallway and change washers. As there were no sons, my sisters and I mowed the lawn and washed the car. We spent Saturday afternoons at the rugby and occasional weekends on my grandfather's farm.

We grew up encouraged to voice our opinions. Exposed to politics and economics from birth, debating and heated arguments were a regular part of my childhood. Family gatherings were never polarised by sex or spent discussing childraising. They were, and continue to be, forums for passionate discussion where members, irrespective of sex or age, fended for themselves.

While I was at primary school and the women's movement was at its peak in the mid-70s, my home life complemented learning and vice versa. In fourth grade, I wanted to be a judge, my friends the prime minister, doctors, and astronauts. Assisted by teachers, girls and boys were encouraged to express themselves as individuals and to try everything as equals.

This situation, however, changed drastically when I went to high school. Females and males were segregated for sport and craft, and in subjects like maths and science, the males dominated the classes and the teachers' attention. Worse, and the most devastating aspect in my eyes, was the change that occurred in my female friends. They began to suppress themselves, and increasingly their actions and thoughts were dictated by the eternal question: "But what will the others think?", "the others" primarily being male. In English, they abandoned science fiction, producing instead bad sonnets pondering love and roses. The astronauts decided to become secretaries and hairdressers, and hours were spent consuming romantic fiction and discussing children's names.

Finally, by third form, I'd had enough. I, along with one or two other female students, had continued to exert myself in commerce and maths, and I was gradually becoming more and more ostracised. I spent much of my fourteenth year in states of depression, continually asking myself if I was somehow abnormal or, more to the point, if my home life was at fault! Because I questioned the traditional roles played by females and males, because I saw myself as an individual and aimed to have a career long after I was thirty, I "enjoyed" a mixed reaction of respect and hostility. While my friends began to "go with guys", I was regarded as somehow different, unapproachable.

The following year I changed to a private girls' school, first as a boarder and then as a day pupil. In the segregated environment, where private lives were separate from school concerns, I discovered sanity again. While there were girls who pictured their future in terms of marriage and motherhood, those of us who didn't were not only accepted but encouraged in our ambitions. I made friends who had aspirations similar to mine, who questioned the traditional role of women, and spurred by the works and autobiographies of women like Rebecca West, Collette and Miles Franklin, I worked on being a writer, a journalist.

Looking back, I treasure my time at the co-ed schools and believe they were instrumental in helping me assimilate. However, I believe that segregated one sex schooling, by and large, is far more productive in achieving more fulfilled lives as independent individuals for girls. The absence of males, and the suppression of girls that results from their presence, allows girls to express their ideas and opinions freely. Single sex schools offer a haven for girls where issues and concerns relating specifically to them can be discussed. While there is still, unfortunately, a tendency in girls' schools both private and public to focus on male achievements in areas like music and art, history and literature, the single sex school offers wider scope for women's achievements, both individually and collectively, to be considered and discussed with sincerity. Female ideas are not treated as trivial and the achievements of women such as Vida Goldstein and Margaret Mead are held up as examples of the capability of women to disregard society's traditional roles.

In my final year, for example, I was able to write an essay on women in Irish history for a unit looking at the background to modern Ireland, and to research and deliver a class paper for General Studies on lesbianism. We also had specific periods set aside for discussion of issues like female sexuality, sexual harassment, and for teaching us to survive after school, the latter in a manner which did not presume we would marry. Our headmistress was especially inspiring, being unmarried and in her forties and having achieved various academic awards.

Perhaps it is not surprising then that in my final year my feminist consciousness reached a peak. Not only did I feel more capable as an individual but I began to realise that subtle sexism pervades our society and discriminates against women — "old boy" networks, and sexual harassment, for example. As leader of the school, I made conscious efforts to bring these aspects and other examples of discrimination to the attention of other girls in the school, something that was encouraged by the teaching staff.

The growth and peaking of my feminism paralleled a re-awakening and re-emerging of my grandmother, following the death of my grandmother's husband the year before. Like countless other women of her generation, my grandmother had, for forty years, found her existence through, and for, her husband and daughters. She had accepted, unquestioningly, the role of mother, wife and housekeeper. However, when my grandfather died, she discovered she had to deal with financial concerns and house maintenance, tasks my grandfather had always undertaken. Due to the developments which occurred in both of us during this period, we have become quite close and she has been particularly influential in my life since leaving school. I greatly admire her and the other women of her age who have overcome internal conflict to re-emerge for life in the 1980s. The feminist movement can be enriched by such women for they have seen and undergone a life of changes. Born when the legacies of the Victorian era still lingered, they were our age in the Depression, young mothers in the war, and lived through menopause watching their daughters criticise the ideas of society and themselves, ideas they had always accepted.

Since my grandmother was a child, single parents, divorce, and pre-marital sex have become more prevalent and socially accepted. I find that this change in values rather questions the institution of marriage and the concept that for every woman there is, somewhere, a "Mr Right". I do not believe in monogamy. People need love from many others in order to fulfil themselves as individuals. No one person can bring out all the characteristics in another. Unfortunately, there is still a belief in our society that a woman's true happiness and fulfilment depend on finding a partner, preferably someone of a similar social background and age as herself — male, of course! Marriage is still viewed as the first step to raising a family and is surrounded by romance.

I have never dreamt of a white wedding and view marriage as a contractual agreement between two equal partners. As far as "love" goes, it is possible to love other women, as well as older and younger people and people from vastly differing social backgrounds. The trouble, however, lies with society. Too many people worry themselves over the morals and lives of others. As a feminist I recognise the right of everyone else to live individually as their own perceptions of self-respect and self-conscience dictate.

I am currently aiming for a future in journalism and writing, and I certainly don't intend to give that up to raise a family, keep house and depend on a man for my survival. In the past, too many women writers have had to choose between writing and "home duties". Of those women who did achieve acclaim as writers, almost all were childless and many remained unmarried — Miles Franklin and Jane Austen, to mention just a couple. For those women who combined motherhood and writing, society tended to regard their work as an interest, supplementary to their traditional role. Fortunately, this is beginning to change, but women in writing, both as authors and subjects, face many dilemmas.

Of prime interest is the role women are creating for women in their novels, the way feminists are portraying women. While male writers in the past tended to stereotype women as weak, subsidiary characters, feminist writers, while placing women in central roles, are tending to concentrate on the internal, introspective problems women have to fight within themselves. While only time will tell, could it be that we are merely changing the stereotype but still perpetrating the portrayal of women as victims? Similarly, women writers have tended to occupy themselves with writing about women for women, not only in fiction but in areas like history. For example, women historians have written books on the achievements of women in a particular era instead of a book discussing the whole era from their own individual feminine perspective.

The experiences of women in major events like war, and in life in general, are different from men's. Our society, however, relies on the research and works of males to educate our youth and our community. Unless women begin to write for this broader audience and unless they are accepted and encouraged not only by critics and educators, but more importantly by other women, the male perceptions of society will be perpetuated. Stereotyping, labelling and images will not change. Discrimination and sexism will continue. The achievements of women will continue to be either ignored or treated as trivial or exceptional.

Women have a right to write. Their experiences are important, their opinions priceless. As writers (and readers) we must assert ourselves and our ideas. We must not continue to apologise for novels that don't deal with power struggles and wars, but we must believe in our right and our ability to use assertive straightforward language and structures to express ourselves. Virginia Woolf, in *Angel in the House*, "kills" the woman within her who taunts her as a writer, who demands she be kind and compassionate. Virginia realised that following the Angel's advice would only lead to bad sonnets that pondered love and roses. As a result, she ignored it and wrote as herself, the individual.

Writing is, of course, only one field in which women have not only a right to participate, but an essential and important duty to involve themselves. However, an increase in the volume of women into non-traditional roles will be worth nothing if we, as women, do not support each other. If we fight amongst ourselves over images and the technicalities of feminism, then we will be deceiving ourselves as feminists. We will be defeating the essence of feminism itself: for feminism is independence. It is individuality. And if, as women, we cannot accept and support one another as the individuals we are, what hope have we of achieving a more united, equal society where individuals rather than conformists are in the majority?

CHAPTER TWO

Employment

Men monopolize ... the most advantageous employments and such as exclude women from the exercise of them , by the publicity of their nature, or the extensive knowledge they require ... Another heavy discouragement to the industry of women is the inequality of the reward of their labour compared with that of men, an unjustice which pervades every species of employment performed by both sexes.

Priscilla Wakefield,
Reflections on the Present Condition of the Female Sex, 1798

In the case of men, their occupation is their life's vocation; in the case of women, their occupation (beyond the domestic sphere) is, in most cases, transitory ... It is not that women are not conscientious; they are often pathetically so. If there is a dreary, monotonous task to be performed, which needs constant and minute attention, it is found that a woman's service is unsurpassed. It is not that women are not intelligent; individual women have again and again in various branches proved their worth. It is not that women are physically weak, individually they may be stronger than individual men, and, at any rate, physical strength is no longer the greatest factor in industry. Women are inferiors in the industrial world because they have not decided (except individually) that they desire to be otherwise, or at least that they desire to pay in training the price of efficiency.

Jethro Brown,
Printing Trades' Case, 1918
South Australian Industrial Reports

Hypocritical insistence that opportunity is really equal is the cruellest form of discrimination. It implies that the loser in any contest has lost through her own inabilities. And while women and blacks realize that the cards are stacked against them, they are compelled by the prevailing rhetoric to act as if they had actually lost out in fair competition ...

Economically, the most elementary demand is not the right to work or receive equal pay for work — the two traditional demands — but the right to equal work itself.

Juliet Mitchell,
Woman's Estate, 1971

The idea that women are inferior to men is nowhere more clearly articulated than in debates on women's right to work. Women are seen as having a *duty* to work (without pay) in the housewife-mother role. Because it is not paid, but "done for love", it is classed as non-work. The right of women to work for money, particularly in areas traditionally dominated by men, is not universally recognised. When women are necessary to the paid economy, such as in wartime when men are absent from the ordinary world of male work, they are welcomed by employers, and propaganda urges them to "do their bit" in the factories and on the farms.[1] In times of economic recession, or when peace is declared and men return from the front, pressure is applied to urge women back to the hearth to fulfil the traditional female role. Yet despite the ideological stand that women don't work or shouldn't work (for money), like most men, most women have spent at least part of their lives in the paid workforce.

In past eras, the jobs reserved for women were always lower paid than jobs reserved for men. Women worked in the fields, did seasonal work like fruit picking, and worked in the mines until "protective" legislation was introduced to keep women and children out and leave mining as "men's work". (The impetus behind such legislation was two-fold: some advocated it to ensure that jobs were available for men; others fought for it on the basis that women and children should no longer be exposed to the inhuman conditions of the pits.)[2] When women attempted to enter more lucrative fields of employment like the trades and professions, obstacles were placed in their path.

Today, as in the past, a frequently voiced opinion is that women are incapable of working in certain areas, that girls' and women's capabilities and talents are concentrated in the non-science, non-mathematical fields. The implication — and often the expressed view — is that women should not strive to be philosophers, electricians, engineers, corporate or tax lawyers, plumbers. If girls and women have the same abilities as boys and men, runs the argument, then ". . . where are your female Beethovens, where is your George Bernard Shaw, your Bertrand Russell, your Plato, your High Court Judge?".

That no woman sits on the High Court bench is not a reflection upon Australian girls and women; rather, it is a reflection upon our (mostly male) lawmakers. From 1788 until the early twentieth century women were precluded from practising law, which alone could have qualified them for elevation to the ranks of the judiciary. Until the passage of *Legal Practitioners Acts* in the various states, women could not be admitted to the Bar, nor become solicitors. After the fight to enter universities was won, women had to fight again to gain admission to professions and trades. The view that women should not be allowed to join the male ranks was based on judicial reasoning. One court, faced with women demanding entry to the medical profession, stated that women had always been excluded from judicial office, for "good reason", and should similarly be excluded from medicine:

> It is a belief, widely entertained, that there is a great difference in the mental constitution of the two sexes, just as there is in their physical conformation. The powers and susceptibilities of women are as noble as those of men; but they are thought to be different, and, in particular, it is considered that they have not the same power of intense labour as men are endowed with ... to some extent, I share this view, and should regret to see our young females subjected to the severe and incessant work which my own observation and experience have taught me to consider as indispensable to any high attainment ... A disregard of such an inequality would be fatal ...
>
> Add to this the special acquirement and accomplishments at which women must aim, but from which men may easily remain exempt. Much time must, or ought to be, given by women to the acquisition of a knowledge of household affairs and family duties, as well as to those ornamental parts of education which tend so much to social refinement and domestic happiness, and the study necessary for mastering these must always form a serious distraction from severe pursuits...[3]

Women's demands did not cease simply because they were refused the right to enter the professions. But they had to work to change laws, not because the laws said only men could become doctors or lawyers or tradespeople, but because the laws used the word "persons", and did not stipulate that that included women! Women became doctors when the *Medical Practitioners Acts* were changed to specifically include the

word "female". And that keeping women out of the professions was based on discriminatory attitudes towards females is
clear from the terms of the debate. Despite changes to *Medical
Practitioners Acts*, in Western Australia, as in other states, the
Legal Practitioners Act 1893 said that "any person" who
possessed certain qualifications was entitled to be admitted to
legal practice by way of articles to a solicitor (a lawyer's
apprenticeship). Edith Haynes had her articles registered by
the Barristers and Solicitors Admission Board and took the
preliminary examination. There was no acknowledgment that
she had a right to do so; rather, the Board exercised a
benevolent discretion. In a letter written to Edith Haynes, the
Board said:

> With reference to your application for admission as a law
> student, the same has been approved by the Board. I am
> directed, however, to warn you that although the Board is of
> opinion (with some doubt) that women are eligible for
> admission under the *Legal Practitioners Act*, yet the Board
> cannot guarantee such admission, even if you comply with
> all the provisions of the Act and of the regulations framed
> thereunder. It must be distinctly understood by you that you
> accept all risk of the Court eventually refusing your applica-
> tion.[4]

When she sought to take the final examinations, Edith Haynes'
wish was refused. In 1904 she applied to the Supreme Court for
permission. The court held that there should be express notice
given in the *Legal Practitioners Act* that women were intended
to be included in the word "persons" in the Act. As "persons"
was not defined in the Act as including women, her application
could not succeed. One judge said:

> I think that the right of a woman to be admitted [to practise
> law] is a misnomer ... The Common Law of England has
> never recognised the right of women to be admitted to the
> Bar ... It appears to me that we must ... bear in mind that
> throughout the civilised [*sic*] world, so far as we know, we
> have not been able to ascertain any instances under the
> Common Law of the United States which is based on the
> Common Law of England, or of any instance in England or
> any British-speaking Colony where the right of women to be
> admitted to the Bar has ever been suggested. That being so,

it is said here that it should exist, because the words in the Statute are "every person". That does not appear to me to be very forcible. The counsel representing the applicant said that there were lady doctors, why not lawyers? The Medical Act says, "Every person, male and female, may be a doctor". Those are different words to what are used in the Legal Practitioners Act. I am unable to find any instances where any right has been conferred. It is not a Common Law right. It is a privilege which has been conferred by the Courts originally, and then been regulated subsequently by Statute from almost time immemorial, and which has been confined to the male sex. I agree with what has been said by my learned brothers, and I am not prepared to start making law. When the Legislature in its wisdom confers the right on women, then we shall be pleased to admit them . . .[5]

The judges stressed the enormity of any proposition that women might become barristers, which would lead inevitably to their being eligible to "sit on this bench". None of the three judges was prepared to make any ruling which would result in any woman having the opportunity of, eventually, becoming his "brother" judge.

By 1921, every jurisdiction in Australia apart from Tasmania had passed Acts allowing women into legal practice. The belief on the part of courts continued to be significant, however. They demanded that every step should be taken doggedly and exactly by women to assert their right to take up professional training and practice in other areas. Thus, in *In re Kitson*[6] Mary Cecil Kitson, a woman, had been duly admitted as a practitioner of the Supreme Court of South Australia, and was engaged in practising law. She applied to be appointed a Notary Public. The court conceded that on the evidence before them there could be no doubt as to the ability of Mary Kitson to perform the duties and exercise the functions of a Notary Public. It said that "the only question is whether the court is, on account of her being a woman and not a man, precluded from granting her the appointment". The *Female Law Practitioners Act* 1911 was considered not sufficiently wide in its terms to give authority for her appointment as Notary Public, because it related merely to the admission of women as barristers, solicitors, attorneys and proctors. The court therefore looked at the wording of the *Public Notaries*

Act; it used the words "every person". The court said that as the word "person" did not include women, Mary Kitson could not be admitted as a Notary Public.

One of the arguments used against women was that married women were clearly not persons. In *Ex parte Ogden*[7] the court ruled that under the doctrine of coverture "a married woman was not a person in the eyes of the law". It looked to the jurist Blackstone who stated that upon marriage, husband and wife became one — and that one, the husband. Even if a woman was single, the doctrine of coverture created problems: what if a single woman was performing the duties of a Notary Public and was suddenly swept away by her knight in shining armour, and married? Suddenly, she would become a non-person. This would create problems for the Notary Public's clients, and should not be tolerated. Even the passage of *Married Women's Property Acts* did not make any difference, according to the courts. These Acts were passed to relieve married women from some of their marital status disabilities. But in *Ex parte Ogden* Justice Hannen declared that the relevant *Married Women's Property Act* was intended to protect married women's property rights, and "was not intended to extend in any way to the political rights of women":

> ... and we must not by a side wind give an extension to its effect which we can clearly see was not intended ...

Employment discrimination against women

Apart from having to change laws to have women included, women have had to fight against laws that specifically state they should not be employed in certain jobs, or that special rules attach to their employment status. Thus, in the 1930s laws were passed stating that women teachers should give up their positions to men.[8] Sometimes laws stipulated that on marriage women had to resign; either they had to leave the teaching service or the public service altogether, or they were employed in temporary positions only. This had negative effects. Drawing distinctions between married and unmarried women made women direct their anger at each other, rather than directing their anger at the members of Parliament who passed the legislation. Married women were depicted as selfish for wanting jobs and not giving younger women or those who

were "too unattractive to catch a man" an opportunity to take
the few jobs available. The idea was also promoted that men
were really the only persons worthy of holding permanent paid
employment: most women would marry, so their jobs were not
regarded as important to them.

Because women occupied temporary positions after they
married, whilst men continued in permanent jobs, women
were less likely to climb the career ladder. In the teaching
profession and the Public Service, temporary employees were
ineligible for promotion. Only by promotion could an employee gain a position of authority, with consequent prestige
and other benefits. In the state and Commonwealth Public
Service, women were prevented from developing their careers
by an additional method: they were excluded from selection
tests for admission to the Third Division in the Public Service
from 1915 to 1949, and from the Second Divisions in the state
services — it is from these divisions that officers are promoted
to high ranking jobs.

For women in the blue collar area, laws and regulations
were equally discriminatory. *Factories, Shops and Industries
Act* provisions and regulations in all states kept women out of
certain jobs.[9] They prevented women doing overtime, working
at night, lifting certain weights. Women were excluded from
labouring jobs, such as working on the roads or doing repairs.
On the surface it appeared that these rules were for the benefit
of women. However, on inspection, that was not the case. The
jobs women were not allowed by law or regulation to perform
were better paid than those they were allowed to do. In some
relatively low paid jobs, such as nursing, women had to lift
substantial weights; yet in jobs where men worked and the pay
was higher, weight provisions kept women out. Often, weight
provisions had no relationship to the work, yet this did not
mean that the regulations were ignored and women given the
jobs (and the wages). The rules precluded women from
promotion: labouring jobs were a necessary step to driving a
crane or other equipment; driving a crane was a necessary step
to the position of manager or foreperson. Thus, managers and
forepersons were inevitably men! Many of these laws remain in
force.

Discrimination exists on a less explicit level, too. Sometimes
employers have drawn up rules which do not have force of law
but are applied nonetheless to preclude women from particular

areas of work. As the *Wilenski Report* into the New South Wales Public Service stated:

> Occupational and functional sex-typing, rather than being legislatively required or biologically necessary, rests largely on the beliefs about the occupations which are appropriate to women and to men ... [10]

Some employers advertise in stereotypical terms, placing advertisements in "men's and boys' " or "women's and girls' " sections of newspapers. Often, requiring an employee who will undertake stenographic duties and some executive functions, a business may call for a "girl friday". Job notices refer to "tradesman" or "salesman" instead of "tradesperson" or "salesperson", except where discrimination law now precludes this. And despite the passage of sex discrimination, equal opportunity or anti-discrimination legislation, employers continue to believe that women are appropriate as workers in certain occupations, while men are suited to others. Even where job applications are called for and interviews held on the basis that women and girls, men and boys have an equal opportunity to be placed on the short list, and to be hired or promoted, conventional views intercede. Women are culled out of short lists, or, reaching the short list, are not appointed to "male" jobs, because employers believe that they will not be suited to the job, or that the appointment of a woman may cause problems. Many employers are reluctant to place women in supervisory positions, regardless of their qualifications.

These problems are compounded by women's and men's views of themselves. Women have been socialised into believing they are not competent as mathematicians or are unable to perform in science classes, apart from biology or physiology, and as a result their job opportunities are restricted. As Diana Forward points out, women are constantly relegated to second place as nurse, not doctor, secretary instead of manager; people assume she is a hairdresser, as this is seen as an appropriate occupation for a young woman. At ten years old, Fiona Giles saw herself as a person in a white lab-coat, but at the same time she acknowledged the existence of another figure in her mind, that of the white-laced, billowy-veiled bride, which seemed to preclude a career. For her, the lab-coated personage was far clearer — but only because of strong family influence which brought home the need for her to see her life in individual terms rather than the expected, conventional wife and mother role. Mary Gartrell comments that she originally wanted to be a teacher, nurse or air hostess, as she was influenced by what she saw on television and the jobs she heard about. Her father's and brother's involvement in science and mathematics ultimately led her to those areas — but she was fortunate. Many girls are firmly socialised, without relief, into accepting stereotypical pictures of women and men: the idea that only a man may become a dentist and a woman his assistant, a man may become a lawyer and a woman a legal secretary, or, today, if it is accepted that women can appropriately function as lawyers, the picture persists of the male corporation solicitor or the high-flying male barrister, with the woman doing conveyancing work or appearing in the Family Court. The image predominates of men entering occupations where dirtiness is a risk (and high pay assured), becoming engineers, mechanics, train drivers; women must enter occupations where cleanliness (with low pay) is the key. A Public Service manual, used as a teaching tool until it was withdrawn in 1978 after pressure from feminists, illustrates this well:

> Make the most of your face and figure. Achieving this can be lots of fun, and it is up to you to make the end result attractive, natural, and worthy of attention. Looking feminine is an art which, if you develop it, can be one of the keys to your happy, successful existence. It has been said that the wise woman regards being good looking and as attractive as possible an essential part of her job of being a "delectable creature" of charm and magnetism ... Receptionist is your chosen career — be a credit to yourself, by always looking your best ... good grooming, graciousness and charm play an important part in the success of the receptionist for the Public Service ...[11]

When Emel Corley listed her job preferences as first, motorbike mechanic; second, motor mechanic; and third, nothing; she was told they were unrealistic and would have to be changed. She writes:

> [When I had] a mechanical aptitude test ... much to the consternation of all those ... who had tried to push me into hairdressing, my results revealed above average mechanical ability.

The work-of-equal-value debate

Today, "a top secretary can earn from $20,000 to $25,000 a year ... The catch is that employers at this level will expect more than the traditional secretarial skills of shorthand and typing", according to the New South Wales manager of a large personnel agency, who was reported in *The Sydney Morning Herald* on 29 March 1984 as saying that the economic recovery "is producing a renewed demand for trained secretaries":

> We now have a lot more jobs than people ... [Secretarial work] is recognised much more as a profession — secretaries at top level are personal assistants to their boss, assessing each piece of paper that comes into the office and dealing with matters that do not need to go to the boss ... They will compose letters, liaise with management and staff, and organise their employers' timetable ...

But, is the remuneration given equal to those tasks? Does the secretary, whose workload may be immense, responsible, and in effect often involve standing in for the boss, gain the prestige and power of her employer? The boss's salary? Equally importantly, does the secretary have a clear career path to follow, or is the "top flight secretary" destined to remain "top flight" — on $20,000 to $25,000 a year, without opportunities for advancement to an executive title and executive salary?

One of the problems facing young women — and older women — is that they have not been taught, generally, to think in terms of career pattern, nor of the necessity to receive payment equivalent to the work done. As Jennifer Stott writes, she now cannot believe that anyone would ever reject the opportunity to take up a university scholarship (her mother did this in 1956, opting to join the paid workforce to save for a home). Jennifer has career ambitions, although she does not see them "in terms of a line upwards". Diana Forward, determined not to take "second place" on the career ladder, has not made up her mind about the career she will enter. Many young women similarly leave their options open. Taking this approach may mean women lead more interesting and fulfilling lives. Equally, however, it means that women remain in secondary roles to men who *have* made up their minds at a relatively early age that they will strive for a particular career goal — whether it is to become a crane driver (with consequent promotion to a supervisory position or other skilled work), or a lawyer (with the opportunity of becoming established in the corporate world, gaining a judgeship, earning thousands of dollars as a barrister in the tax field ...), or an electrician or fitter and turner (resolving to own their own business in the future).

Payment equivalent to the job done is an important principle. Yet, many women do not recognise the value of the talents they possess. Nor do they understand that their work is downgraded relative to men's, with a resultant downgrading of remuneration. Others, like Mary Gartrell, are aware that males get paid more than females, and register that fact as indicative of work-based injustice. Like Michele Trewick, they know that "women have to work harder" and "men work only half as hard" to succeed in the paid work world. But despite women agitating strongly for equal pay for equal work, "equal pay" is not a reality.

As the Women's Electoral Lobby pointed out in its submission to the 1983 National Wage Case before the Australian Conciliation and Arbitration Commission, despite the Commission's decisions aimed at implementing equal pay for women and men, women's and men's wage levels remain discrepant:

> From June 1976 to March 1983 award rates of pay for males rose by 84.6 per cent. For females that figure was 83.6 per cent. [But] when we consider *actual earnings* of females relative to males (not just award rates of pay), a less encouraging picture emerges. Rates of pay may have moved in parallel, but the gap between male and female earnings remains ...
>
> In 1972 females earned 65 cents for every dollar earned by males. By 1975 that figure was 76 cents. After an initial improvement that ratio has levelled out to about 78 cents in the dollar.[12]

The difference between rates of male and female pay is even more pronounced when part-time workers are included. Only twenty-five per cent of women are in fulltime paid employment. When part-time workers are taken into account, "female earnings are further depressed": from a position of earning sixty cents for every dollar earned by a male in 1972, in 1981 the figure was sixty-seven cents. "In short," said WEL,

". . . there is still a gap between men's and women's wages."
The reasons for this are threefold:

- there are barriers to the implementation of equal pay
- the Equal Pay Decision of the Australian Conciliation and
  Arbitration Commission is being circumvented by some
  employers
- there is a systemic imbalance in the labour market

Evidence shows that where under-award payments are made to
workers, women are more likely to be the recipients: a survey
by the Amalgamated Metals, Foundry and Shipwrights' Union
(AMFSU) in 1980 showed these differences between female
earnings and male earnings:

- five dollars per week or more in fifty-one per cent of cases
- ten dollars or more in forty-three per cent of cases
- twenty dollars or more in eighteen per cent of cases

WEL commented:

> The [Australian Conciliation and Arbitration] Commission
> says that all jobs in this class are worth the same rate of pay.
> Over award payments may account for some of the
> differences. Allowances may also account for some of the
> differences. It may be in this case that female process
> workers don't do jobs in which allowances are paid.
> Allowances and over award payments may account for some
> earnings differentials. However, some differentials can also
> be accounted for by what appears to be under award
> payments to female process workers.[13]

Of 15,720 process workers in an AMFSU National Wages Survey, 7.8 per cent of male process workers received under-award
payments, while 17.8 per cent of female process workers
received less than the award wage in 1980. In a later AMFSU
survey, no below-award wages were paid to male process
workers, but below-award wages were paid to approximately
ten per cent of female process workers. Allowances and mar-
gins for skill, applied along sex discriminatory lines, also result
in a circumvention of the Equal Pay Decision.

Another means of escaping the requirement that women
should be paid equal rates to men is by reclassifying jobs. Following the Equal Pay Decision in 1972, jobs were reclassified

along gender-based lines. Where women and men had previously worked alongside each other, or on the same or almost equivalent tasks, women were regrouped into areas where no men worked and set to work on tasks classed as exclusively "female"; men were regrouped and set to work on tasks classed as exclusively "male". Certainly, prior to the Decision, men worked mainly in "men's jobs", and women in "women's jobs", but demarcations were emphasised by employers to avoid paying women the equivalent of men's wages in areas where they might be obligated to do so. In some cases classifications were drawn up and women placed on lower classifications than men, whatever the tasks women and men were actually engaged in.

This led to a reorientation of the demand for "equal pay" to that of "equal pay for work of equal value". That is, the principle changed to dissecting the tasks involved in a particular job and comparing these with tasks carried out in jobs done by men for higher pay. The underlying premise, however, was that only tasks of a like nature should be compared. Are the tasks done by women comparable with any tasks done by men? Margaret Thornton comments in the *Journal of Industrial Relations*:

> The significant gap between men's and women's wages in Australia has been reinforced by sociological, economic and judicial factors. The implementation of the principle of "equal pay for equal work" has done little to remedy the inequity for the majority of women in the workforce, who are engaged in sex-segregated occupations, because they have not been considered to perform "work of the same or a like nature". Analysis of the *Universities (Equal Pay) Case* illustrates, however, that the introduction of the broader principle of "equal pay for work of equal value" is undermined if applicants still endeavour to demonstrate that women are engaged in work identical in nature to a predominantly male classification. Such an approach is inappropriate in the case of women clerical workers since the number of men involved in keyboard and transcription work is miniscule. This work has become stigmatised as *per se* inferior and as justifying a low rate of pay regardless of other administrative duties performed.

An "equal value" case should be able to be framed in such a way that the work of women in female-dominated occupations can be compared systematically with that of men employed in discrete male-dominated occupations in the community in respect of education, training and expertise required.[14]

Although work value enquiries have been carried out on male occupations, resulting in upgrading of pay for jobs done by men, work value enquiries on work done by women, to upgrade rates of pay in their jobs, have not been carried out to the same extent. In fact, WEL noted in its submission to the *National Wage Case* that during the three-year period 1977 to 1979 very few women participated in work value cases:

In the year 1978, one married woman at Rockhampton won a test case establishing the right to work irrespective of marital status; one woman in South Australia was granted pro rata long service leave after ten years' service with an insurance company, thereby setting a precedent; nine thousand ancillary workers in New South Wales, all women, gained half pay for about ten weeks a year during school vacations, when previously they had received no pay. Amongst [all] the cases ... the only women involved apart from the ancillary workers were some process metal workers who had their over-award pay indexed and an unknown number of workers in the Food Preserving industry who received an over-award payment.[15]

To overcome inertia or resistance to women gaining wage justice, WEL requested that, in addition to a return to centralised wage fixing, the Conciliation and Arbitration Commission endorse three proposals that:

- all female occupations immediately be made the subject of work value enquiries
- provision be made for an adequate and effective mechanism to provide for restructuring of work assessed by reference to work value criteria
- provision be made for an adequate and effective mechanism to provide for special and extraordinary circumstances based on anomalies and inequities to be taken into account in the restructuring of work

WEL considered that each award coming up before the Commission for variation should, as a matter of course, be subject to a work value enquiry where women's work was involved. Assistance from government and the Commission should be forthcoming to unions to enable this to be done, and a panel of commissioners should be established within the Commission to concentrate upon work value enquiries for women's occupations. WEL endorsed the ACTU proposal that inequities and anomalies cases should be recognised by the Commission for wage increases where:

> In addition to similarity of work [with another, higher paid occupation] there exists some other significant factor which makes the situation inequitable. An historical or geographical nexus between the similar classes of work may constitute a significant factor.

The history of women's work shows clearly that women have suffered differential treatment in the workplace. This differential treatment cannot be ignored today, because women's contemporary position is directly and indirectly influenced by past disadvantages and the perpetuation of myths about "a woman's place". The history of women's work is a crucial factor where adjustments are proposed to wages within the centralised wage fixing structure.

Despite the case put to the Commission, WEL's requests were refused on the ground that any massive reevaluation of women's work would upset centralised wage fixing. This is ironic, because it in fact recognises the degree to which women have been cheated of adequate and appropriate remuneration in the past, and confirms an attitude that women should continue to be cheated of their rightful wage, thus preserving women's wage injustice. Furthermore, despite the Commission's stating that other propositions put to it could come into operation two years after the reestablishment of the centralised wage fixing process, it did not support the introduction of any procedure, at that later date, whereby a wholesale reevaluation of women's work could be undertaken. It did not recognise that in failing WEL in this way it had condemned women to continue as before, without work value being taken seriously where women's occupations are concerned.

Changing the work face

Attempts are being made by state and federal governments to improve girls' and women's chances in the paid workforce. The methods used are two-fold. First is the provision of opportunities to simply gain a paid job, through the allocation of community employment programme moneys and "wage pause" funds on the basis that fifty per cent of the jobs thereby created *must* go to girls and women. (In unemployment figures, girls constitute the highest group, in February 1984 registering 31.9 per cent of unemployed compared with 27.1 per cent of boys unemployed. The figures for unemployed women are deceptive: many women fail to register and therefore are not included in the statistics.) The second method is anti-discrimination, equal opportunity and sex discrimination legislation operating federally and in South Australia, New South Wales and Victoria, with Western Australia scheduled to introduce such legislation. Affirmative action legislation is in effect in New South Wales in relation to public sector employment and is under consideration at federal level. Equal opportunity laws aim to ensure that girls and women have equal access as boys and men to all occupations and to remuneration commensurate with their job. Affirmative action laws and programmes are designed to ensure that girls and women are equipped with training and skills to enable them to compete equally with boys and men for jobs and salaries. Special programmes are introduced for girls and women, and training in non-traditional areas is encouraged.[16]

In the Hunter Valley industrial area in New South Wales and in Victoria in the industrial belt of La Trobe Valley, governments have worked to make non-traditional jobs accessible to girls and women. In particular, governments have initiated apprenticeship programmes on the basis that girls should be encouraged to apply. The aim is, in Mary Gartrell's words, to create a paid work world where "normal" women do a wide range of jobs. For Michele Trewick, living in Queensland with the benefit only of federal initiatives for equal opportunity (the Queensland government has not introduced sex discrimination legislation and sees no necessity for it), it is important to ensure that all occupations are equally filled by women and men. And as pointed out by Keith Windshuttle, in the current economic climate:

> ... the only youths who can be confident of long-term,
> career employment are those who gain some form of post-
> school qualification in a technical college, CAE or univer-
> sity. The youths who go looking for jobs straight from
> school, no matter how well they might have done in the
> School Certificate or Higher School Certificate will find
> fewer and fewer places in the workforce.[17]

Girls and boys have to gain equal access to training at all levels,
and provision has to be made for programmes that will provide
worthwhile work for those who are not able to specialise or take
part in skills training.

However, changing the work face is not so easy. As a
subsidiary argument to that with which it ruled against the
Women's Electoral Lobby work value enquiry proposals in
the National Wage Case, the Australian Conciliation and
Arbitration Commission stated that any such procedure
"would ... be inappropriate in the current state of unemployment especially among women".[18] As both Jennifer Stott
and Cathy Henry recognise, during any economic downturn
women's job conditions are threatened; their very right to
occupy paid work roles, and particularly to occupy them on an
equal basis with men (never given full community support) is
more at risk. Apparently the Conciliation and Arbitration
Commission subscribes to this inequitable situation.

Ann Game and Rosemary Pringle comment in *Gender at
Work* on the effects of economic downturn on employment,
noting that women lose jobs and men move into women's
traditional areas, forcing women out.[19] Although in many
industries overall numbers of workers have been reduced,
women have been eased out of paid work more so than men.
Jobs have been "deskilled" in many areas, but this has not led
to any influx of women into the "easier" occupations. Game
and Pringle describe a press shop at a factory in South Australia where numbers have fallen from 120 to roughly thirty.
Although less physical effort is required than previously,
because the work is now done at the push of a button, the men
have retained the jobs on the basis that they are exercising
power over machinery, making it a male preserve.

Where they take over "female occupations", men (or employers) have the job description changed to give it a masculine connotation. In *Brothers — Male Dominance and Technological Change*, Cynthia Cockburn reports:

In times when jobs were many, industries were expanding and technology was creating more jobs, in different areas (rather than as now, rendering human workers, as far as possible, obsolete), the problem of "men's jobs" becoming more like "women's jobs" would be solved by men removing from the area ... leaving [the work] to the women, recovering their masculinity in some other expanding area — with "danger", "dirt" ... and higher pay. Today, to hold on to the dwindling number of jobs, despite their "feminisation", the traditional solution [is] to redefine "male" and "female" work.[20]

In the press shops of the whitegoods industry, which are defined as "male" areas, larger presses were occasionally operated by women, but mostly by men; women also sometimes operated smaller presses. With jobs declining, women have been forced out of the press shops, or more rarely left operating the smaller presses in smaller numbers. The reason? One employer reports the women are afraid of the presses! At Kelvinator, new presses were introduced which did away with any distinction between large and small. The solution? It was attempted to remove women from the area altogether, going so far as to seek to gain an exemption under the South Australian *Sex Discrimination Act* on grounds that sex discrimination in the press shops was lawful, due to sex being a "genuine occupational qualification". In the compositing industry, Cockburn found men resented women joining "their" workforce; they saw women as a problem. Computerisation of the industry meant "more women will come in, yes, and to me this is a bad thing", said one worker. Another claimed "there is a resentment about girls [sic] coming into the industry. It is a threat, a definite threat ..."[21]

Just as it is important to provide role models for girls in the education system, placing women in positions of authority in all areas and promoting women to upper levels in all professions, trades and jobs generally, it is equally essential that efforts be made to change male and female attitudes and behaviours. It is not sufficient to promote the idea that "girls can do anything", placing them in apprenticeships in non-traditional areas or encouraging them to enter male-dominated professions. Support networks must be provided in those areas too. As Emel Corley found, training to become a motor mechanic was difficult because all her fellow students were male; they were deliberately unhelpful and unwelcoming to her and, eventually, physical violence was used against her. Her own determination to succeed was bolstered by support from women's groups outside the technical college in Brisbane where she trained. In the workplace, she confronts sexism daily. Cathy Henry, studying law in New South Wales, similarly sees a need for regular support group meetings of women in non-traditional areas, both during training and in the professional world.

Support groups for women are necessary not only to preserve women's self-confidence in their ability to do the job as well as men, but also to give them confidence in any unique talents they possess. As one woman architect has said, it is ironic that although women spend a greater part of their lives in the home than men do, almost all houses are designed by men. She graduated from Adelaide University in the 1960s, one of only two women. She comments:

> They pushed my feminine design creativity out of me. I lost track, just concentrated on passing exams. It took me seven years to get back to designing buildings which were *mine*.[22]

Although the composition of architecture faculties is changing, with almost half the first-year students in architecture at universities in New South Wales and Queensland being female, it is not enough to depend upon sheer numbers. Male dominance has been so strong for so long that additional efforts are necessary to overcome "masculine thinking", teaching, and action on the job.

Trades training, technical colleges and universities must be required to incorporate courses which acknowledge the contribution of women. Although there are not as many female as male architects, lawyers, medical practitioners, motor mechanics or plumbers, it is important that trainers and teachers use examples of women's work alongside those of men. Men in the trades and professions must be brought into contact with the reality that women are equally capable of performing in those areas and are equally often exceptionally talented.

At the same time, women training and working in traditional female areas should not be left without support.
Women working in those areas suffer sexism on an equally
large scale as those in the non-traditional . The secretary who
has been conditioned into accepting that her role is one of
hand maiden to the boss is faced constantly with a denigration
of her abilities: stenographic work is not seen as skilled work by
men and organising a boss's schedule and coping with clients
are most often viewed as menial tasks, despite the important
influence a secretary's skills — or lack of them — may in fact
have on business deals. In New South Wales the spokeswoman
scheme has done much to raise women's consciousness about
their place in the workforce and to lift their perception of their
rights. (Each government department, or sections of a department, elects one woman to act as spokesperson, liaising with
the departmental head or a highly ranked officer on issues of
concern to women in the department or section.)[23] Although
some of the issues raised may not appear to be important to
outsiders, the value in the scheme is that women are able to
build a picture of themselves as an integral part of the Public
Service and as contributing significantly to the overall work of
the agency. They begin to see that they are not isolated, and
that other women work with them and suffer similar problems
They can talk about issues which otherwise might go un-
remarked. Problems of sexual harassment or being passed over
for promotion can be brought to the fore. Women who have
never considered they have a right to promotion, or the ability
to perform in higher levels, are encouraged to apply. Women
who have not believed they have a right to protest against
exploitation by superior officers — whether it be sexual
exploitation or simple abuse of authority — begin to see that
being at a particular level in the hierarchy does not mean that
they have to suffer such abuse. Women can encourage other
women to take up studies, or continue with studies where they
are discouraged.

That women are able to get together to discuss these
matters is important also for changing men's attitudes. That
women begin to see themselves as legitimate operators in the
workforce, with equal rights to their male fellow officers, may
have a salutary effect. Because time is allotted for spokes-
women meetings, and because the spokeswoman representative
has access to the departmental head or high ranking officer,

further legitimacy is given to women and women workers' concerns. Private enterprise should be encouraged to introduce similar schemes to complement affirmative action policies and programmes.

There are encouraging signs in the workplace for women. These signs are not enough, however. Affirmative action legislation is necessary to ensure that private and public enterprise cannot simply assert they are operating in accordance with principles of equal opportunity, without being required to show clear evidence of this. Under affirmative action laws, all enterprises would be required to undertake yearly audits of "where women are" within the organisation. They would be required to set goals or targets, to look at the numbers of women and men in the company, department or agency; contrast these with numbers of women and men in the community who are qualified to take up particular positions within the organisation and then outline programmes for ensuring that women are promoted to positions for which they are qualified.[24] As a complement to this, organisations should be required to provide training programmes for women to ensure that a minimum number gain the skills necessary for promotion to higher positions.

As Michele Trewick puts it, women must fight many more years to gain equality in the paid workforce. And at the same time, women have a right to expect men to put in an effort — although this will be far more difficult to bring about: in the short term, men can expect to lose the privileges they have enjoyed through the oppression of women; in the long term, changes in the workplace are calculated to advantage both women and men, in that no one's success will be dependent upon the unequal treatment of others. Ultimately, it cannot be denied that girls and women have a right to develop and realise their (too often secret) hopes for careers and paid work. In the past, women were discouraged from articulating their career ambitions. Today, young women like Emel Corley can say, without fear that no one will understand or fail to applaud their stand: "I hope one day to have an all women's garage." Tomorrow, those ambitions should be as realistically attainable for women as for men.

Emel Corley

Emel Corley, *twenty years of age at the time of writing, was a third-year apprentice motor mechanic. She had been involved in the women's movement in Queensland since she was fifteen.*

My parents are strong Catholics who were born and bred in Queensland. They have lived in Queensland all their lives and in spite of it all are surprisingly tolerant and considerate of other people's "differences". I am the youngest of their three children and was always considered to be the "tomboy", fix-it person, and general hand around the house. There was little choice, as my older sister was generally obscured by books and my hyperactive brother would be running around the neighbourhood somewhere. This all made for a remarkably independent and risk-filled childhood — risks like those encountered in climbing the roof of our high-set house to clear the guttering of dead leaves and refuse. I escaped my household duties as often as possible, usually in the company of other young refugees from domesticity.

When I was about twelve years old my sister became involved in the women's movement. At first I was repulsed by her missionary zeal, particularly her strident efforts to "raise my consciousness". We talked lots about sexuality and the roles men and women are forced to live, and I came to realise that my beliefs fitted comfortably with feminist ideology. Over the following years I met many of my sister's friends and became more involved with feminists and political activists. Then, the civil liberties campaign for the right to march in Queensland was at its height and I began to attend demonstrations.

Finishing school at the end of year ten I decided to leave home. My sister was living in a communal house with other women and I moved in with her for a short time. When my parents' fears were allayed, I moved into a house with two other women. These friends were communists as well as feminists. One of them in particular was to influence me greatly.

The year I left school I began a pre-vocational trade-based course at Eagle Farm Technical College in Brisbane. Even getting to this stage was a battle of wits against obstructive careers officers and bureaucrats in the Commonwealth Employment Office. At the employment office I was told that my job preferences — listed as (1) motorbike mechanic; (2) motor mechanic; and (3) – — were unrealistic; they would have to be changed. Working Women's Charter members picketed the employment office. I was eventually allowed to keep my original preferences.

Senator George Georges heard about the incident and arranged for me to have a mechanical aptitude test. Much to the consternation of all those paternal careers officers who had tried to push me into hairdressing, my results revealed above average mechanical ability. I applied to the pre-vocational trade-based course which teaches basic principles in most trades — fitting and turning, bricklaying, carpentry, mechanics, electrics, sheet metal work — and counts as credit towards an apprenticeship.

Later I discovered the college had an affirmative action system of selection: ten per cent of positions were reserved for women, ten per cent for black Australians, ten per cent for the disabled, and the other seventy per cent for boys. This is a well-kept secret. I was the only woman who applied to the course, out of 750 applicants (which was probably because I was the only woman in Brisbane who knew the course was available to us) so I got in straight away.

I was the only woman in the company of 150 adolescent boys.

They had done between two to four years of woodwork, metal work and technical drawing at school. I had done two years of typing and shorthand. When the boys realised I was good at my work and didn't rely on them to carry things for me or favour me with their chivalry, they began to make life difficult. Boys constantly tripped me up and down stairs, threw food and soft drinks at me and put gum in my locker so I couldn't get my books out (making me late for classes). They smashed my carpentry and bricklaying. Then, on the way to the train station, they'd throw stones at me.

School was horrific. I'm sure I would have abandoned the course if not for collective action taken against the boys. Women friends decided to see how brave males were when faced with a group of women instead of me alone. About thirty women met the train from college. We grabbed the worst offenders, pushed them around, and questioned them about their continued harassment of me. They were terrified and tried to scramble across the platform to their next train. There was no attempt to fight us as a group. It was every man for himself. After their defeat, they made up stories exaggerating our toughness: they were confronted by a bikie gang arriving with crowbars and chains. This about a group of women — teachers, students, social workers, my mother, public servants and unemployed.

I was moved to another class. They were to be my "protectors" on the instructions of the principal who had questioned me about the train station incident. To me, this showed how little the college understood. They dehumanised me by saying I was in need of protection, then appointed my potential attackers to the position of protectors.

Finishing the course, I came second in my class. At graduation I was ignored by the principal and teachers: they commented only on how well the boys had performed.

I went overseas. When I returned to Brisbane I found an apprenticeship as a motor mechanic, but not without trouble. Prospective employers could not ignore my good results, but neither could they ignore my sex. It took me six months to find an employer who was prepared to employ a woman.

I have never fitted very well into the submissive feminine stereotype. In that way I suppose dormant feminist traits were always there. My moment of awakening came when I was doing the course at technical college. The harassment was directly related to my being a woman, and being a woman who wanted to do something different. I realised then how much I needed the support of other women. Thinking about it now, five years after it happened, I can hardly believe I was able to withstand the pain and complete the course.

Now, apart from my working hours, I spend most of my time with other women. Apart from individual activity with women, I belong to the Young Women's Collective in Brisbane. Primarily a consciousness-raising group, we are all under twenty-one years old. I began my group activities in London in 1980 in a young women's group, and earlier with the Working Women's Charter in Queensland.

I can't remember even thinking about marriage as a child. By the time I was a teenager I had been exposed to ideas about alternative relationships. Marriage was outside my expectations or desires. Now, I don't see marriage as necessary. It is merely a shackle on what might seem to be a good relationship. As a feminist I agree that marriage is one of society's instruments for the oppression of women. A woman loses her independence — clearly evidenced in the loss of her "maiden" name. Married women are seen as second class citizens. They are the first to be sacked in economic recessions and they cannot claim unemployment benefits.

For the last five years I have been living in various communal houses with other women and sometimes with children. I enjoy this living arrangement and don't see why it should not continue indefinitely. Having my own child might happen, but it is not important to me. Presently I am sharing a house with two other women and two young children. I enjoy their company and believe it is vital that more than one adult should take responsibility for care of a child. A child should feel security and love from stable adults in their lives. The sex of the adults is unimportant.

The women's movement has changed people's beliefs about roles women and men should adopt in society. Today it is more acceptable for women to take up careers like medicine, law, and journalism. More opportunities are generally available to women in education and career choice. However, it is unfair that women should still be faced with the question of career versus family. Men never face the question. Women should have the choice of using free childcare, provided by the government on a round-the-clock basis. Living in group households would also alleviate the childcare problem.

Of course my own experience reveals acceptance of women in career roles does not extend to all areas of the workforce. Women have an increased awareness of their personal worth and rights as human beings. I think women are also more aware of their sexuality, with greater freedom to enjoy its expression.

Even so, we still have a long way to go. Ideally people should not be treated differently because of their sex. Women and men should have the same opportunities and responsibilities in education, career choice, relationships and childraising. Feminist action has taken us a good way in this direction. Feminism is to me the most important issue; it affects my life daily. My lifestyle allows me to confront sexism. Issues such as world peace, land rights and the like are vitally important. I support these causes by attending demonstrations and rallies. But at present I do not feel the same attraction that draws me to feminist issues.

For myself, I hope one day to have an all-women's garage.

Cathy Henry

Cathy Henry, *born in Newcastle in 1961, was studying law at the University of New South Wales when her piece was written. She intended to specialise in poverty law and anti-discrimination law.*

Moving towards a feminist ideology has, for me, been a very gradual process. In some ways, I still have ambivalent feelings. I have trouble identifying with some strident radical feminists, yet at the same time find myself constantly having to defend women and the feminist position against sexist attacks and constant ridicule from many men I know.

My family background has been conducive to education. It has been a major influence both on my choice of career and ulti-mately on my development as a feminist. This has been more of an unconscious process than a reaction on my part in sup-port of, or against, the views of either parent. For most of their working lives, my parents have taught at universities. My younger sister, brother and I grew up in a house full of books where learning of some description always seemed to be going on, whether our parents' research or our homework. We were certainly a very studious lot!

While I was never conscious that either parent was particularly ambitious for us, they were encouraging and always willing to help us with our work. They spent a great deal of time discussing career options with me during my last years at school and I think it was always assumed that I would go to university. During these impressionable years, I remember my mother constantly reminding me that she believed girls should not feel pressured into marrying and having children, reinforcing by implication the importance of a career.

As long as I can remember, my mother has pursued a career outside the home. She is now a lecturer in history, after spending fifteen years as a tutor, and in 1978 completed a Master's degree begun many years earlier. Her example has encouraged me to pursue a career, whilst at the same time making me aware of the difficulties of combining a career and family. In retrospect it seems that her career has always been subordinate to that of my father and to the interests of the children.

Although housework was never my mother's favourite pastime (something I must have inherited from her), she nevertheless assumed responsibility for the running of the household. She clearly regarded traditional domestic tasks, with the possible exception of cooking, as a waste of time. We were all expected to help out, which was useful when we left home. My father also helped with domestic chores, especially when we were young, but there was never an equitable sharing of domestic responsibilities, which undoubtedly left him comparatively free to get on with his career. He has a Ph.D. and was until recently a senior lecturer in engineering.

My mother's involvement in a wide range of community activities which probably did little to advance her career and which led my father to call her "Causes Incorporated", may have influenced my attitudes, although I have previously been reluctant to admit this. When I was growing up she was involved in the anti-Vietnam war movement and in Aboriginal affairs. She has been an active member of the Australian Labor Party for many years and I have done my share of letter-boxing at election times. Although she would now describe herself as a feminist, she has only become active in the women's movement in the last couple of years. She has always been interested in the elderly and is now doing research in that area.

While my family (especially my mother) has been a major influence on my views and my development towards a feminist position, I have also been influenced by some women at university who appear to me to have "got it all together" as regards a successful combination of career, marriage and child-rearing roles. They have influenced me more than feminist writers or public figures. I would hope in the future to be able to emulate their apparently well-balanced lifestyles.

Although aware of the difficulties in combining career and marriage, I would hope to make a success of both. I realise the importance of marrying someone who would respect my wish to continue working after marriage and would be prepared to share equally in child-rearing and domestic roles. In Australian society in the 80s, I know such men are a rare breed. I am hopeful that attitudes are beginning to change, however slowly.

I suppose that up until recently, like many other women, I have been prone to talk of marriage as some sort of inevitable, almost unavoidable, future event. In my experience, many women will talk of marrying, despite the absence of any long- or short-term relationship with a man. In our society, the pressures on women to marry seem to come mainly from parents and the peer group, and to be reinforced by the media.

These pressures appear to differ according to the community in which the woman lives. If I had stayed in Newcastle, my home town, I might have felt pressure to marry. A number of my schoolfriends who stayed there to train or work have married boyfriends from school and are now saving for homes and furniture and planning families, while in the years since leaving school I have been preoccupied with coping with university work and supporting myself with part-time jobs. I do not envy my friends or feel pressure to emulate them, nor do I imagine they envy my lifestyle.

In the past few years I have been living with large groups of students in a communal situation. While I have enjoyed it, I would not choose to live this way indefinitely. I don't think I would like to live with a boyfriend in such a communal situation. It could create strains in the relationship and tensions within the household. More importantly, it would inhibit my freedom and independence. If I was contemplating marrying, I would prefer to live with the person for some time before marriage. I would hope that this would give us both time to see whether we were compatible, although I realise it is still an artificial situation. I would not agree to a longstanding de facto relationship, because I think women are legally and financially vulnerable in such a situation. I am also conscious of the vulnerability of older women when a longstanding de facto relationship breaks down.

Of all the alternatives as I see them, I would ultimately have to express a preference for marriage. To me, marriage implies a commitment by both parties which may increase the degree of stability in the relationship. With children, I would prefer to be married to the father, as I believe it is important for children to have a continuing relationship with their father.

Although I concede that combining marriage and career would be possible only in a marriage where the male did not feel threatened by an independent woman, I would like to think marriage and a feminist lifestyle are not incompatible, or even antagonistic. However, I am not as confident about combining a career with childbearing and rearing. Although I don't like all children, I would like to have my own. My family life has been happy, by and large. I now enjoy a good relationship with my parents and, in spite of the inevitable clashes, get on reasonably well with my brother and sister. I am aware of the challenge to the concept of the nuclear family, but my own experience is that I prefer it to the alternatives.

I am sure I would find it difficult adapting to the role of fulltime mother. My own mother has never idealised her child-rearing experience and has insisted women should have a choice about marrying and having children. I would want to continue my career and would find it stultifying to be deprived of stimulation through working in my profession and being confined to the house with small children, for long periods. For my own, my children's and my partner's sake, it would therefore be essential that we share all domestic responsibilities, especially child-rearing, in a real, not a token manner. Failure to share in child-rearing deprives men of valuable life experience and places close relationships with their children at risk. It leads also to resentment and tension in the relationship. An agreement on the division of labour between partners should be reached before marriage.

Continuing with a career would also require recourse to childcare services. A good supply of high quality care is essential. Existing services are hopelessly inadequate. They are relatively elitist, catering mainly for the middle class and the wealthy. My own memories of a rather authoritarian kindergarten make me want something better for my own children. Even with such childcare, I realise the difficulties of combining family with pursuit of career. Irrespective of these reservations, I intend to make a career in law.

Whatever the views of my friends when I was at school, I saw continuing my education at a tertiary level as an almost natural progression. I was influenced by decisions of some of my school friends to embark on similar courses as they, and also by my parents. They encouraged me to consider alternatives to the traditional female professions.

My school was supposedly the best selective school for girls in the area. The absence of boys was possibly a contributing cause of the quite high proportion of girls doing traditionally "male" subjects, including a sizeable four-unit maths class. Our careers adviser, a highly efficient, extremely forthright woman, who kept us well informed of a wide range of career choices, was also an influence.

Between school and university, I spent a year working and travelling in England and Europe. Much of the year I worked in menial jobs, traditionally the preserve of unskilled, uneducated women. My motivation to go to university increased considerably. Living and working away from home for the first time and travelling alone on the continent increased my self-confidence. It helped me to decide on the arts/law course at New South Wales University.

Looking back, I'm pleased with this decision. The arts component has furthered my interests in politics and social issues. The law course has a reputation for innovation and progressiveness and, while providing training in the compulsory hard-core subjects, has also provided me with the opportunity to study more socially orientated subjects such as discrimination, housing and welfare law, choices not available in some other major law faculties. My preference for these areas of law was confirmed during my recent period of employment in a large city law firm. Further, working at Redfern Legal Centre and, through the clinical legal education programme, at Kingsford Legal Centre, has given me practical experience in the same areas.

In my five years of university I have continued to work to support myself in a wide range of casual jobs — shop assistant, waitress, cleaner, and most recently as housemaid in an hotel where one of my jobs was to scrub urinals! As when abroad, working with women in boring, usually dirty, and predominantly badly paid jobs has contributed to my awareness of the disadvantaged position of women in the workplace and to my development as a feminist. Now I am in my final year, I'm clear about the sort of work I want to undertake.

My evolution as a feminist has not, then, been the result of a "moment of truth". Indeed, not so long ago I can remember expressing hostility towards my mother's comparatively mild interest in feminism, which she manifested by listening to *The Coming Out Show* on radio. I described it as "stupid feminist crap". Why did her latent interest in feminism upset me? I'm not sure, but I may have been reflecting my father's unease about feminism; I may have perceived it as a threat to my parents' relationship.

Until fairly recently I was busy conforming to the female stereotype, which appears to please men, as far as appearance and attitudes are concerned. This may have been a by-product of a reaction to my years of attending a single sex school, but was more likely to be a defensive reaction to hostile comments from men about feminists — their supposed unattractiveness and "unbecoming" aggression, and ribald speculation about their sexual proclivities. When I gained self-esteem and read feminist literature as part of my course, I was able to retaliate, countering these barbs and attacks on feminists and women generally. Many men I know still seem to view feminism as some sort of threat. As a result, I think women are afraid to admit their sympathy for the feminist position, for fear of ridicule and because they believe it will place their relationships at risk.

It is therefore essential for women to be supportive to each other, to counter this hostility. This supportive role is an important aspect of feminism. Certainly, female friends are very important to me. When I have enjoyed a close relationship with a man, I still feel it is important to maintain friendships with women. I don't like to be dependent on a man or men for my social life, and frequently go out with female friends. I resent the patronising implication of the "girl's night out" reaction of many men to a group of women. Some women's company I enjoy, as I do that of some men. In times of stress, my women friends have been very supportive. At the same time

I endeavour to be supportive of them if they are going through a similarly difficult stage in their lives.

On a collective basis, I have not really had time to become as actively involved in women's groups as I would have liked, because of demands of work and university. I am a member of the Women's Electoral Lobby, and the newsletter keeps me informed on feminist issues. However, I have been inhibited by an apparent "generation gap" in the membership. There is a need for younger women to become more actively involved in such groups. It is particularly important for female members of professions, especially those like law which are male dominated, to meet regularly, providing a support network. The Feminist Legal Action Group (FLAG) and Women Lawyers undoubtedly fulfil this role.

In law, as in most professions, there is still a long way to go before women are adequately represented. This does not deny progress already made in a number of fields, where in recent years there has been a steady influx of women. In 1983, there were seventeen women members of federal Parliament elected. In the state elections in Western Australia, immediately preceding the 1983 federal election, there was a similar and even more dramatic result — where previously two women had sat, six new women members were elected, and one returned.

In increasing numbers women are entering other so-called male professions — medicine, law, journalism, engineering and commerce are, perhaps, the most obvious examples. In trades a similar trend is apparent, largely resulting from government measures and the collective action of women themselves. Other government initiatives have gone some way towards improving women's status — for example the creation of women's advisory councils and introduction of anti-discrimination legislation in some states, and at Common-wealth level by the Labor government. In New South Wales the Wran government has been particularly active. It has developed and maintained a policy of appointing women to boards of hospitals and councils of tertiary institutions, and has legislated for equal opportunity and affirmative action programmes in the Public Service.

Women's initiatives have been important. The worldwide involvement of women in the peace movement has a strong counterpart in Australia. Aboriginal women are increasingly involved not only in the land rights campaign but also in other fields, notably education. That the current head of the New South Wales' Department of Aboriginal Affairs is a woman, Pat O'Shane, is illustrative of this new development. Women have always been active in ethnic affairs also, and are increasingly so. As well, the lobbying of feminist action groups for reform in areas of vital importance to women has had good effect. Their efforts have meant not only that the feminist position has been publicly articulated, but has ensured a considerable degree of feminist input into crucial legislation. The recently amended sexual offences law in New South Wales is a good example.

Nevertheless, despite these changes, there remain areas where women are disadvantaged. The most glaring example is women's continued oppression in the workforce. In the present economic climate, women are especially under threat with their increasing concentration in part-time and casual jobs, and the continuous campaign against married women working. With the rundown in social services, characteristic of the Fraser government years, there has been considerable pressure on women to continue, and increase, their role as voluntary labour, whilst maintaining their traditional responsibility for the care of children and elderly relatives, with minimal support.

The position of women in society will continue to be disadvantaged while it is the *exception* for women to occupy positions of authority and responsibility in the community. We need more women judges, more women at the Bar, more women editors, more women principals in coeducational schools, more women academics occupying the more senior positions in tertiary institutions ... to name but a few examples. What is needed above all else, however, is a change of attitude. For it is not really until such things as the high incidence of sexist advertising in the media in all its forms and pornography in films and in literature cease to be accepted as the norm — and, indeed, begin to be seen as undesirable — that we may realistically move towards the eradication of sexism in society. To achieve this, women (and men!) need to *dare* to become feminist. They need to be convinced they have nothing to lose and everything to gain.

Marriage

At the present day women are cheap; their value in the great world's market has sunk to a very low ebb. Their attitude, speaking generally, is that of cringing for a piece of bread. What dignity can there be in the attitude of women in general, and toward men in particular, when marriage is held (and often necessarily so, being the sole means of maintenance) to be the one end of a woman's life, when it is degraded to the level of a feminine profession . . . when the insipidity or the material necessities of so many women's lives make them ready to accept almost any man who may offer himself.

Josephine Butler,
Woman's Work and Woman's Culture,
1869, Introduction

Frenchmen have hit upon a unique method of boycotting women from the professions usually held sacred to men. The woman lawyer is fairly firmly established in Paris, but her confreres do not mean her to remain so, for the junior members of the Bar have entered into a solemn league not to propose marriage to any lady who follows a profession which belongs by tradition to the other sex. The movement has been joined by other professional men who are afraid of female competition, and seems to be formed in all seriousness. Apparently it has not occurred to these gentlemen that women who are capable of entering the learned professions would hardly be likely to listen to proposals of marriage from men who so openly confess their weakness and inefficiency.

"Puck's Girdle"
Sydney Morning Herald,
12 January 1910

If economic necessity forces you to be productive outside your home after marriage, you will be taught how to pretend you aren't doing it. If you show any symptoms before marriage of going after a career for any reason other than that of facilitating your search for a man, you are peculiar and eccentric. If you go about saying you want and like to be a Worker you'll be considered dangerous.

Elizabeth Haws,
Anything but Love, 1948

I have a very clear, keen memory of myself the day after I was married: I was sweeping a floor.

Adrienne Rich,
Of Woman Born, 1976

For years marriage has been regarded as the primary concern of young women growing up. Girls were brought up to believe that they should regard marriage as a career; their fulfilment would come with wifehood and, later, motherhood. Yet this was a romanticised vision of marriage, having little to do with the realities. It ignored the diversity of abilities possessed by young women. Often, it blinded women to their ability to achieve in other ways. Furthermore, economic necessity meant most married women spent time in and out of the paid workforce. Marriage as (sole) career was never an option for most. Husbands died or deserted leaving their widows destitute unless another husband appeared to take up the breadwinner role. Even where husbands were major breadwinners (and some were not), women were obliged by need to participate in contributing financially to the household. If no husband was forthcoming, or if following desertion or death of a first husband no second husband arrived, an alternative to marriage-as-career had to be found.

Today, a new romanticism surrounds marriage: the idea that marriage is a "contract" between two equal partners. Is this any closer to reality than the earlier vision? Dominant modern ideas remain distant from pre-medieval man-woman relationships which were more likely to be founded on greater equality of the partners. The medieval and post-medieval influence of laws and mores remain influential in present society, both in relation to laws and to attitudes.

Before the medieval era, marriage was not controlled by the church and the state. Indeed, marriage as we know it today — bound by laws, confirmed by church ritual or state ceremony — did not exist. For the "common people" in particular, mating was a matter of two people living together, no doubt with the blessing of their families in most cases, as well as the approval of friends and other relatives. But no necessity was seen for church or state involvement.

However, marriage became an important means of economic and social control with the growth of property ownership, the amassing of fortunes, and the development of a mercantile class. In Europe the law of marriage was consolidated and defined for the upper classes early on. The court of the Archbishop of Rheims set a judicial pattern for other courts to follow. Secular and ecclesiastical aspects of marriage were outlined in 860:

> We learn from the fathers and find it handed down to us by holy apostles and their successors that a marriage is lawful only when the wife's hand was requested from those who appear to have power over her and who are acting as her guardians and when she had been betrothed by her parents or relatives and when she was given a sacerdotal benediction with prayers and oblations from a priest and at the appropriate time established by custom was solemnly received by her husband, guarded and attended by bridal attendants requested from her nearest kin and provided with a dowry. For two or three days, they should then take time out for prayers, guarding their chastity, so that they may beget good offspring and please the Lord. Then their children will not be spurious but legitimate and eligible to be their heirs.[1]

Laws continued to control women by way of the marriage relationship throughout the medieval period, placing a woman in the control of her father until she passed from him to the control of her husband. The law of dowry played a large part. In Italy Ragusan women were legally defined by "the extensive and highly specific laws governing dowries", Susan Mosher Stuard records in *Women in Medieval Society*:

> While her rights to a dowry outweighed the rights of her brothers when she reached marriageable age, her dowry marked her final legal claim on her parents, as prescribed by Roman tradition. At marriage she passed to the custody of her husband or the head of her husband's household, insuring that she be a private rather than a public person all her life. If her husband's debts came due in his absence she was not held responsible; rather, a term was set for her husband's return so he might answer the debt himself, and a relative might answer a debt for a woman as well. In fact, following the principle established by the Roman jurist, Ulpian, in the third century, a woman was represented by a male advocate if it became necessary for her to appear in court.[2]

As well as the control of women, marriage laws were designed
to ensure that men of fortune could pass their property down
to their male heirs without fear that an interloper would
succeed to it. Women's activities were strictly policed, so that an
illegitimate child could not be foisted upon an unsuspecting
husband. Efforts were also made to ensure that women could
play no part in decisions about property. Upon marriage, they
lost all their rights to property ownership. Even where there is
some evidence that women exercised legal rights despite being
married, and although the law stated that their legal rights
were subsumed in those of their husband, this exercise was not
for their benefit but for the benefit of their families. Stuard
comments that in some cases it was possible to find a woman
appearing in court for herself, contrary to the stated law. She
says:

> The failure to amend [the law to conform to this reality] in
> the case of women may lie in the fact that only a few women
> behaved in a manner contrary to the spirit and provisions of
> the law, and then only in the interests of the family.
> Consequently it was in the interest of the mercantile class to
> make exception or ignore the law in certain specific cases
> rather than amend it.[3]

She cites the case of Nicoleta de Mence, who left her husband's
home, taking with her those goods she had brought into the
marriage. Although there had been instances where married
women were named in legal documents and appeared in court
when goods they had brought into marriage were transferred
to other parties, the court in the *de Mence Case* did not
acknowledge that Nicoleta de Mence had a right to leave her
husband, nor to take "her" goods with her, to appear in court,
or to be represented in court when her husband brought an
action against her to have her return to him — with the
property. Stuard sums up:

> The *Libri Reformationes*, despite the cryptic nature of the
> account, reveal a concerted effort on the part of the Small
> Council [the court] to avert the severity of the law in
> Nicoleta's case. But her husband continued to bring suit,
> and he had the law on his side. Nicoleta had no right to
> deprive him of her dowry or her person, and there the case
> rested. The law might be stretched or ignored to further the
> interests of family business and the larger interests of the

mercantile class; it could not accommodate to a woman's demand for her individual freedom . . .[4]

Social attitudes underlay the legal position, and reinforced it. The role of the wife was to obey, standing as she did in a much inferior position to her husband — legally, politically, economically and socially. During the medieval period, tracts and tomes were written in the form of letters from a husband to his wife, admonishing her to do all that was good and proper and wifely, so to do him credit. Such an epistle was that of *The Goodman of Paris*, written in the late fourteenth century, where an older husband addressed his wife as "dear sister":

> You being the age of fifteen years . . . promised me to give all heed and to set all care and diligence to keep my peace and my love . . . beseeching me humbly in our bed . . . each night, or from day to day, in our chamber, to remind you of the unseemly or foolish things done in the day or days past, and chastise you, if it pleased me, and then you would strive to amend yourself according to my teaching and correction, and to serve my will in all things, as you said. And your words were pleasing to me, and won my praise and thanks, and I have often remembered them since . . . For your youth excuses your unwisdom and will still excuse you in all things as long as all you do is with good intent and not displeasing to me. And know that I am pleased rather than displeased that you tend rose-trees, and care for violets . . . and dance, and sing; nor would I have you cease to do so among our friends and equals, and it is but good and seemly so to pass the time of your youth, so long as you neither seek nor try to go to the feasts and dances of lords of too high rank, for that does not become you, nor does it sort with your estate, nor mine . . .[5]

The treatise goes on to outline nineteen principal articles covering various aspects of married life, as dictated by the husband. His wife should at all times follow them. She should be "careful and thoughtful of [her] husband's person". He prays that she should "keep him in clean linen, for that is [her] business". When any husband is away on business, continues *The Goodman of Paris:*

> . . . he is upheld by the hope that he hath of the care which his wife will take of him on his return, and of the ease, the joys, and the pleasures which she will do him, or cause to be

done to him in her presence; to be unshod before a good fire, to have his feet washed and fresh shoes and hose, to be given good food and drink, to be well served and well looked after, well bedded in white sheets and night-caps, well covered with good furs, and assuaged with other joys and desports, privities, loves, and secrets whereof I am silent. And the next day fresh shirts and garments ...[6]

Considerably more in this vein follows, with admonitions that there are three things which "drive the goodman from home, to wit, a leaking roof, a smokey chimney, and a scolding woman ...". Therefore a wife should keep herself in good cheer, good temper and at all times be "unto [her husband] gentle, and amiable, and debonair". The "goodman" tells his young wife how to keep fleas from the bedchamber and her bed (there are six ways of effecting this), and how to keep the flies out of the chamber:

Item, have your windows shut full tight with oiled or other cloth, or with parchment or something else, so tightly that no fly may enter, and let the flies that be within be slain with the whisk or otherwise as above, and no others will come in.
Item, have a string hanging soaked in honey, and the flies will come and settle thereon and at eventide let them be taken in a bag.
Finally, meseemeth that flies will not stop in a room wherein there be no standing tables, forms, dressers, or other things whereon they can settle and rest ...[7]

He concludes, before setting out an interminable list of menus and recipes she should use, that by doing everything he has said, his wife "will cause [her new husband — who is to follow when the "goodman" is dead and long since gone] ever to miss you and have his heart with you and your loving service and he will shun all other houses, all other women, all other services and households ...".

The English common law adopted the rules created by the ecclesiastical courts during the middle ages. Marriage made the spouses into one flesh — that one flesh was the husband's. This meant a wife had no property or personal rights. On marriage, any property she might possess became the property of her husband. If she was in paid employment, her wages belonged to her husband. Her husband alone had the right to control and manage any land she might have owned as a single woman, and any land her father gave "to her" upon marriage or prior to marriage. The husband received any income from rented properties. He could dispose of them by giving them to anyone. If a woman made a will before marriage, the will was revoked upon marriage and she had no right to leave "her" property to anyone. If she made a gift of property to anyone during the betrothal period and her husband discovered this, he could revoke the gift whenever he wanted to. A woman's personal goods, including her clothes and any jewellery, belonged to her husband absolutely upon marriage. He could do with them as he wished. Any "gifts" he gave to her were not hers; they remained his property because the law considered she had no personhood and therefore was incapable of asserting any legal title to them. On marriage, a husband became responsible for any debts his wife might have. However, if he failed to pay the debts and squandered all the property she had brought to the marriage, then died, the debts reverted to her — and she had no property or money with which to settle them. On death of her husband, all a woman could claim was those ornaments for personal decoration (her "paraphernalia") that he had not disposed of by sale or gift before he died, and any leasehold property that was hers prior to marriage — unless he had given this away or sold it.

A married woman had no right to appear in court. She had no right to bring legal actions against anyone, including her husband. She could not have her husband prosecuted for theft, for she had no property for him to steal; everything he took from her, he took by right. She could not have her husband prosecuted for beating her, raping her, or otherwise abusing her person. These acts were legal.

Married women and slaves were in a parallel situation, and ironically the position of the married woman predated that of the slave. Caroline Norton, fighting in the nineteenth century for her right to property and to custody of her children against a vicious and alcoholic husband who continually defamed her, recognised this clearly. In her *Letter to the Queen* pleading the rights of married women, she alluded to a case tried in the Covington Circuit Court in November 1853 where a slave named Sam Norris, belonging to a Mr J. N. Patton of Virginia "had been permitted to work in Covington, on condition of paying each year a certain sum to his master; which sum was accordingly paid". Then, Mr Patton decided that the slave should buy his freedom with an additional sum. When the sum was almost paid up, Mr Patton changed his mind, rescinding the contract and claiming Sam Norris as his slave:

> The case was argued with much ability; but at the close of the argument the judge decided for Mr Patton against Sam Norris, on this principle, that by the law of Kentucky, "*a slave cannot make a contract, nor can he have monies of his own.*" The contract, therefore, was null and void; and the money, though received and expended by the master, could not be held *legally* to have been paid. The report concludes with this consolatory admission, that the Hon. Judge Pryor, before whom the case was tried, "characterised it as one of great hardship and cruelty; and every one in the court-room seemed to sympathise deeply with the poor negro."[8]

Caroline Norton commented that she most truly shared in that sympathy, but "the case has besides a peculiar interest for me, inasmuch as I find, in the slave law of Kentucky, an exact parallel of the law of England for its married women; and in this passage in the life of the poor slave Sam Norris, an exact counterpart of what has lately occurred in my own".

During the late sixteenth century efforts were made to improve the position of married women. They were not, however, designed to grant married women any rights. Rather, they gained protection for a married woman's father's (or grandfather's) property, so that it could not be squandered by her husband. The aim was to ensure that the woman's sons (her father's grandsons and heirs) would succeed to the property. The purpose was to consolidate large property holdings by keeping them in the family, so that they passed down the male line and continued to increase. However, the law of equity (which tempered the common law position) was for the rich only: equity courts were not interested in intervening if the property involved was less than a hundred pounds, or ten pounds a year (considerable sums at the time). The ordinary woman who did not have a rich father was in no better position. Money she earned in any low paying job she might be sufficiently fortunate to obtain remained her husband's.

At the same time, women were disadvantaged in relation to divorce rights. Few people were able to obtain divorce before the late nineteenth century, for it was necessary to have a special Act of Parliament passed. The only grounds for divorce were adultery by a wife, or aggravated adultery by a husband (the husband's adultery had to involve incest, bigamy, rape, sodomy, or bestiality). Divorce was costly and men had greater access than women, if only because women did not have any money — they owned no property by law. If a woman wanted a divorce, her father or some other sympathetic (male) relative had to pay for it. During the period 1670 to 1857 when the first divorce law reform was passed in England, only 325 divorce Acts were passed by the Parliament. Of these divorces, only four were obtained by women. In Australia prior to divorce law reform, only one Act was ever mooted in the New South Wales Parliament, and this was never passed.[9]

Discrimination in marriage and divorce law reform

During the nineteenth century in Australia, as in England, women fought strongly to have marriage and divorce laws reformed. Their efforts met with some success, although laws remained discriminatory against women. *Married Women's Property Acts* were passed providing that women who owned property on marriage could retain ownership of that property in their own right. Wages they earned became legally theirs. However, any money they might save out of the housekeeping money, because they were thrifty, did not become theirs. It remained that of their husband (as it does today, if it is paid out of a husband's wages). Divorce became more easily obtainable, with grounds such as cruelty or drunkenness being added to that of adultery. But women remained at a disadvantage: the standard for an action for cruelty was set so high that a woman had to endure years of gross abuse before she could obtain a divorce on such a ground; aggravated adultery rather than simple adultery remained the ground for women, while men continued to be able to obtain a divorce for simple adultery. Women suffered greater stigma when divorced than did men, and this further impeded their access to divorce. Women's economic position was less secure than men's, again emphasising disparities between the two sexes in both marriage and divorce.

Attitudes toward women as wives remained primitive. During debates on marital property and divorce law reform, archaic views were frequently expressed by male politicians (by law, women were prevented from entering Parliament). Reform and women's rights became hopelessly entangled in prejudice. One member said:

> It seems to me . . . most extraordinary that my honourable friends are so fond of woman's franchise, and always trotting in the unfortunate women, so that you might almost think that the whole of the women of this colony were treated like beasts and brutes, and that the men were monsters of iniquity all round. We are always having this women's cry dinned into our ears. In point of fact, I believe, as to those honourable gentlemen who are always cramming this cry about the rights of women down our throats — that in their case Nature has made a mistake, and that, instead of being men, they should have been women and have had the petticoats, and that their better halves should have had the trousers. That is my conviction. It is getting nauseous.[10]

In 1959 the *Matrimonial Causes Act* was passed by the Australian Parliament to take over control of divorce from the states. Women and men were able in theory to obtain divorce on equal grounds: separation for five years, desertion for three years, adultery, cruelty and drunkenness were the major grounds. In practice, however, divorce remained more difficult for a woman than a man, due to lack of finances, problems of maintenance arising from lack of access to equally well-paid jobs, or to jobs at all, and social attitudes which continued to discriminate against women. Maintenance was awarded where a woman could show that she was the wronged party. If she left her husband because life with him was unbearable, she ran the risk of being divorced for desertion; in such a case she would not be entitled to maintenance. The high standard of cruelty was retained, so that a woman was placed in the position of having to either endure abuse, or leave and bear the possibility that her husband would lodge a divorce petition against her, or would cross-petition (if she sued for divorce on grounds of cruelty or constructive desertion) and win; again, she would lose any right to maintenance or property. Marriage property laws, although even-handed on the surface, in fact continued to discriminate against women. Few women owned property in their own right. Few women had their name on the title of the family home. Even if they did, the husband could claim that the wife had not contributed any of the purchase price, and that she held her portion in trust for him. Often, newspaper headlines screamed of large property settlements or maintenance claims being ordered by the courts; these cases were rare, however. If a woman did not conform to the accepted picture of the devoted wife and mother, she had no chance of obtaining maintenance or a property settlement. Where maintenance was awarded, it was frequently unpaid, and women had to pay legal fees to obtain advice on having it enforced. Often legal intervention was of no avail; maintenance remained unpaid. Husbands also defaulted on property claims.[11]

Further moves for reform culminated in the passage of the *Family Law Act* in 1975. Under this Act, divorce was to be granted on one ground only, that of marriage breakdown. Husband and wife had an equal right to petition for divorce on this ground. The Act made parents equally responsible for the maintenance of any children of the marriage following divorce, so that maintenance could be ordered to be paid by either parent. Equally, maintenance could be ordered to be paid by a husband to a wife or a wife to a husband on identical grounds: s. 75. Property entitlements were also the subject of reform. The new Act provided for the efforts of the parties in accumulating assets to be taken into account in relation to direct financial contribution, indirect financial contribution, and non-financial contribution made to the acquisition, maintenance and development of property, and contribution made in the way of parenting and spousal "duties": s. 79. Feminist women's organisations, including the Women's Electoral Lobby (which had been involved in advising on the new law), welcomed the changes. The property provisions were regarded as a major advance, providing as they did for women's traditional efforts in the home, as wife and mother, to be taken into account. However, theory and practice are not identical. Decisions of the Family Court and settlements made at the court by registrars soon began to show discrepancies.

And despite the theoretical changes (and some improvement in practice), some young women at least see marriage as an unequal relationship and one which may be, or is, detrimental to women. Jennifer Stott says marriage is not something she sees herself involved with, for many reasons, "not the least that it is an institution with little to offer other than a false sense of security". Fiona Giles considers the marriage contract to be imperfect and historically based on requirements of property ownership rather than individuals' needs. At school, Sarah Gillman was taught about post-school survival, which did not carry any presumption that girls should think of marriage as the means of surviving in the adult world. Now, she continues to question the institution of marriage and the idea that for every woman there is a "Mr Right" waiting to be discovered. In a personal development programme run at Anna Donald's school, one of the topics was marriage and what students thought about it. Most students thought marriage inevitable but, she comments, "with over half the class with divorced parents we could hardly take it as the eleventh commandment that thou shalt get married. It was quite a topic for debate . . .".

Despite these views, most young women continue to want to marry, as do young men — and they do, although not at such a young age as before. Lincoln Day writes in *Violence in the Family*:

> Marriage is still popular. Whatever the press may say, whatever some of the ministries may have said, . . . the overwhelming majority of Australians give every indication of planning to marry legally. However, they are marrying a bit later. Particularly significant in this is the fact that there has been a drop in the rate of teenage marriage. In the five-year period between 1971 and 1976 the male first marriage rate declined by 37 per cent at ages 15 to 19; the female by 30 per cent. At ages 20 to 24 the rate for men declined 27 per cent, that for women by 33 per cent — and so on. In the 30 to 34 year age groups, the marriage rate declined among men by only about 11 per cent, and among women by only seven per cent. [There is] a 66 per cent decline in the marriage rate for women aged 16.[12]

Mary Gartrell writes that she "might consider it today with the right sort of person". Diana Forward says she was always against marriage, swore she would never marry, but doesn't believe it is necessarily incompatible with a feminist lifestyle. For Karen Ermacora, marriage is "acceptable only if people are making knowledgeable choices".

Why these reservations on the part of young women growing up feminist? If young women have no reservations about marriage, are they right in that approach? Although changes have improved women's situation in marriage, legally, women remain disadvantaged by marriage. During this century, women's place in the marriage relationship, at least under the law, has been virtually ignored. Changes in some states have occurred, so that in New South Wales a woman can no longer be raped by her husband with impunity: he can be prosecuted, just as a stranger can be prosecuted for rape. In South Australia the law is more complex and wives are not equally protected from their husbands' sexual abuses. In some states the law of rape operates only where the parties are separated or divorced. Women are also disadvantaged in the application of seemingly equal laws. Thus, although it is criminal for a man to assault his wife, just as it is criminal for a man to assault another man, laws are rarely used to protect female victims of domestic violence. Police retreat from doing their duty, excusing their inaction on grounds that "it's just a domestic".[13]

Social attitudes continue to be dominated by the idea that women should choose between a career and marriage (although this may be changing in some quarters to the idea that married women should choose between a career and motherhood). Despite lip service being paid by some to the principle that men and women should participate equally in the paid workforce and equally in doing the unpaid chores at home and in childcare, studies show that men prefer to marry women who are traditional in their behaviour, and who take upon themselves the major housekeeping and mothering role, whether they are in the paid workforce or not. Yet studies also show that the happiest human beings are unmarried women! (The next on the scale are married men, followed by married women, then unmarried men — which indicates that of the sexes, marriage suits men better.) Research by Faye Fransella and Kay Frost in *How Women See Themselves* also shows that women who are more highly educated are more reluctant to marry — perhaps because they are more aware of discriminatory attitudes expressed in traditional marriage and of the legal disadvantages for women in the married state.[14]

Sex discriminatory attitudes are also evident in marriage and divorce laws where rights to property ownership and income are in question. Although the *Family Law Act* takes into account, in the words of the Act, the contribution traditionally made by women to property accumulation in marriage, while the parties are living together the law does not regard such a contribution as relevant to property ownership. To have it taken into account, a woman has to seek a divorce. In doing so, she need not hope that her contribution will be regarded as equal to that of her husband.

The marriage-versus-women's-rights debate

Diana Forward writes that it is "not marriage itself that oppresses women, at least today ... Instead, it is the way marriage is treated ...". Married women are treated as dependants, despite the reality that women work hard in marriage to build up marital property, hoping to ensure that the family home and business (if there is one), and any other assets will improve in value, providing present security and security in old age. The reality is equality of contribution. As well, women work hard in marriage to maintain a good emotional relationship; frequently they contribute more energy and effort to this aspect than do men: society expects women to contribute more to the emotional side of relationships than men.[15]

The romanticised view of marriage as beginning at the altar with the woman bedecked in tulle and lace, or more stylishly before a marriage celebrant in (usually) glamorous garb prevents women (and men) from seeing the reality. Marriage has economic consequences. Most often, it has consequences which operate negatively on women's autonomy. Today, most women are in paid employment when they marry. Frequently they continue in their job until the birth of the first child. Some then take maternity leave. Many, however, leave work for good (although probably with a vague idea of returning to the paid workforce at some time in the future, when the child or children are at school). Bringing a paypacket into the household gives women the rightful feeling that they are contributing equally to the marriage. With the birth of the child, many women begin to feel they are dependent upon their husbands: it is *his* money which keeps the household going. Yet simultaneously with feeling dependent, the woman in this situation is contributing greatly: washing, cleaning, cooking, dusting, brushing, ironing, changing nappies, feeding children and husband, psychologically supporting family members...

If a woman is in the paid workforce during marriage, she frequently works in a part-time job. Between 1966 and 1982 the main changes in the female labour force included "a growth in the aggregate participation rate from 36.3 per cent in 1966 to 43 per cent in 1975, and to about 44 per cent since then". Most of this increase involved part-time workers, mainly married women.[16] In addition, therefore, to suffering lower pay than men because differentials between male and female pay rates are built into the system, women are likely to earn even less: their husbands are more likely to be in higher paid, fulltime jobs, while women are in lower paid fulltime jobs or lower paid part-time jobs. Because she earns less money than her husband throughout the marriage, many a woman believes she is not contributing equally, at least where property and income rights are in question. Thus, when a husband asserts that any property purchased is "his", or that his wife is living in "his" home, most women believe it. Where they deny it, and attempt to protest their contribution, frequently they feel uncertain about the truth of their claim. They downgrade their participation in building up the property and in creating an environment which makes it possible for a husband to return each day to the paid workforce and bring home the weekly wage.

Even where women are earning more than their husbands, they suffer from dominant social beliefs which ignore the facts. Women are forced to rely on their husband's signatures in order to obtain loans. The New South Wales Anti-Discrimination Board has documented numerous cases where women have been refused loans because they have not produced a husband as guarantor, or the husband has not been ready to take out the loan himself.[17] In a telling feature in *The Weekend Australian* (9-10 July 1983), Vickie Smiles reports the case of Ms Bergere who wished to buy a computer priced at $2500:

> Unable to pay cash ... Ms Bergere approached a finance company ... She was somewhat taken aback by the unusual questions asked ... Was she married? Did she and Mr Bergere own their own home? ...
>
> Ms Bergere had no qualms about providing this sort of

information, although she wondered why the gentleman [at the finance company] wanted to know about her chesterfield lounge suite and Philips refrigerator . . .

The final crunch came, however, when it was time to visit the finance company and sign all the documents. Could she bring her husband and her car with her? . . . Having recorded the fact that the car had been "sighted" the gentleman then ushered Mr and Ms Bergere into his office and pushed the papers under Mr Bergere's nose for signing.

"Hold it!" Ms Bergere said. "It's my computer and I'm paying for it so why should he sign the documents? In fact, I am the main breadwinner in this family and it's me who'll be paying off the damn thing."

This had no effect on the finance company. The article continues:

Spurred on by the deathly silence, Ms Bergere let forth about how, before she was married, she had bought her own home, run a successful business and manipulated her daily finances with great flair. Why then should she suffer the ignominy of finding herself described as a "spouse" on a little bit of paper that had nothing to do with anybody but herself . . .

"This is how we do it madam," the gentleman said. Finally, bored by the whole affair, Ms Bergere decided that if the finance company wanted her to be a "spouse" then she may as well be a "spouse" with a computer.

If during a marriage any woman sought, through a court, to assert her right to half the marital assets, she would rarely obtain a judgement in her favour. Mostly, it is the husband's money that has gone into paying the mortgage, the rates, the bills that relate to buying property, even if all the property owned is a family home, or a car, or furniture. Mostly, it is the wife's money which is spent on consumer items, such as clothing for all family members, food, entertainment expenses, "extras" for the children, Christmas and birthday presents. This means she does not have any legal right to property purchased, although the parties are married and although she is contributing substantially to the wellbeing of the family — including her husband.

At divorce, sex discriminatory attitudes mean that

although such contributions by women are taken into account, and the principle of "equality is equity" or "equality of contribution" should be the rule whatever roles the parties fulfilled during the marriage, the courts' decisions show that the equality principle is not applied in practice. The traditional view of women's work as not being equal to the work of men influences decisions. Women have to live up to a high standard of performance as wife and mother to gain a fair share of the property of the marriage.[18]

Would the problem be solved by young women renouncing marriage as a lifestyle and entering de facto relationships instead? Michele Trewick does not consider this a real option: "living together is useless . . . there is no sense of permanency which is integral . . .". On the other hand, Anna Donald and her school friends consider it important to live with a pro-spective husband for a long time before marriage — if marriage takes place at all. Similarly, Mary Gartrell thinks a de facto arrangement "appropriate . . . as a prelude to marriage . . .". But even as a prelude, or as a lifelong alternative, de facto relationships are problem-filled and may cause more legal difficulties than marriage whilst harbouring as many day-to-day "living together" difficulties as a legally sanctioned union.

In discussing her attitude toward marriage, Jennifer Stott comments that she is concerned about personal space and has a "niggling fear that intense relationships mean the loss of autonomy". Michele Trewick contemplates the possibility of marriage in which both parties maintain their independence, yet she doubts if:

. . . many men would sacrifice the security and pleasure they get from their jobs to get married — yet . . . these same men expect their wives to stay at home and give up their working lives to look after their husbands . . . most men start to look down on their wives as mothers [rather than] spouses and this . . . is a drastic mistake . . .

If marriage is seen as a trap, Michele writes, then it is unworkable. But if a husband understands the needs and rights of women, then there should be no reason why marriage is incompatible with feminism. These fears and hopes are equally compatible with living in a de facto relationship. The problem for young women in contemplating male-female relationships is that the "serving" position women have been required to fulfil, although exaggerated by marriage laws, is seen as necessary for the subsistence of "good" relations between the sexes. The "ownership" idea that historically underlay marriage may be exacerbated by a legal ceremony and the existence of a marriage certificate, but women have no assurance that the absence of these eliminate assumed male superiority.

Most parties living together inevitably accumulate property together. If the woman is in a paid job, she will be earning less than her de facto spouse in most cases. Like married parties, de facto spouses may decide to have children, or children may simply "come along". In most cases, the woman will take the major child-rearing responsibility, frequently placing her earning capacity in jeopardy. As in marriage, if the de facto husband's money is spent on the mortgage or other assets, the property will belong to him. The de facto wife will have no claim on it, whatever her efforts in the home and in caring for him (and any children). Similarly, she will have no claim if her money has been spent on consumer items without any durability, such as the clothes and food ...

If the parties break up, what then? Anna Donald comments that the girls at her school contemplated not marrying, because of the "hassles of divorce". Yet ending a de facto relationship is equally susceptible to difficulties — or more so! The parties cannot go to the Family Court, because the *Family Law Act* does not apply to them. Certainly they do not need to go anywhere for a divorce, but they may have disputes about who owns what property. Custody disputes may also arise. [19] If they cannot agree, the parties must go to the Supreme Court in their state. Generally, the position is that the party putting money into the purchase of property will own that property. The question is, who has formal title in the property? This can be answered by a trip to the land titles office. If both parties' names appear, the presumption is that both parties own the property. If one party's name appears, the presumption is that that person owns it. However, the law of trusts may become relevant — it could be argued that despite both names appearing on the title, one party was holding it in trust for the other. If it can be shown that one party alone paid for the property, then that party can assert ownership whatever the title says.

Because of income differences between women and men, it would be most likely that the de facto husband would own the property, and the court would award it to him.

In *Allen* v. *Snyder*[20] an unmarried man and woman met in 1955 and lived together for thirteen years. They lived in a house registered in the name of the de facto husband. When the relationship ended, the man demanded full ownership of the house and sought to evict his former de facto spouse. The court held that the woman had no right to any of the home, despite her contribution to its maintenance and to her de facto husband's wellbeing, and despite purchase of improvements to the property, and the fact that under the loan agreement he would not have been entitled to purchase the home except for the fact that she was classed as dependent upon him by the agency granting the loan. (The loan agency would not allow her name to appear on the title. Nor did it require her signature to the loan!)

Changing personal relationships

Is it somehow wrong to think about property and income issues when contemplating marriage? Or to talk and write about them as if they are inextricably woven into the relationship? Does it take the romance out of marriage or attempt to turn it into a mercenary arrangement? Should love be blind to financial matters? It might be suggested that property and income matters are of concern only to the wealthy; that those in the lower socio-economic strata are untouched by property problems and attention should be concentrated on matters that are of concern to them. Or young women, like Fiona Giles, may consider that because they do not believe property is an important question — believing perhaps that all property is "evil" and can only become "pure" when owned communally — it is irrelevant to worry about any property component in marriage or similar relationships.

What is of importance, however, is that every person is entitled to personal space — and that comes about with rights of access to property — even if only to "a room of one's own". What is also important is that women do not ignore that marriage *is* a loving relationship — if the parties are truly equal, and have equal entitlements, including equal entitlements to personal space. It is difficult to sustain a loving relationship if parties are inherently unequal, and if money matters loom large because the parties have not considered them prior to marriage. It is equally difficult to sustain a loving relationship if one party is constantly concerned about whether she is pulling her weight in a marriage, or worried about whether the family finances are being wasted. Additionally, it is untrue to suggest that any married people, however poor, do not have property which has potential for creating disagreement, stress and strain on the relationship. Even if it is only a television set or an electric frying pan, or in these days of more readily accessible finance arrangements, a microwave oven, married or de facto partners care about who has a right to what. Indeed, where the property owned is less, the concern of the parties may be even greater. And even if everyone lived in a communal environment, disputes about use of property could arise, calling for laws which ensure that all parties have equal access and equal rights with regard to it.

It is essential for young — and older — people to recognise that when living together, whether in marriage or in an alternative relationship, questions about property, income and finance generally will be important. Sometimes they may be less important than others; some marriages or other relationships may well proceed calmly without any disputes over financial matters. However, all individuals must recognise the potential for such disputes. That is why it is essential to have fair laws which treat women and men equally, so that in those cases where parties are unable to agree in amicable fashion, it is possible to go to court and to be sure that just treatment will be dispensed. Relationships may be happy, with *never* a word said about assets, yet, realistically, such relationships must be rare.

Can people evade legal problems in personal relationships by setting out their intentions and rights in a contract? Under the *Family Law Act* it is not possible to oust the jurisdiction of the Family Court in this way. If a husband and wife write up a contract and disputes arise at marriage breakdown, the court has the power to override any agreement that the parties have made. If there are disputes during the marriage, the Supreme Court in each state would be entitled to interfere in the terms of the contract. If parties are living in a de facto relationship, it is not clear that any contract they draw up will have the force of law. Thus, if there is a dispute and the parties go to the Supreme Court to have the dispute settled, the court will not necessarily take the written agreement as the final say. In 1982 in *Seidler* v. *Schallhofer*[20] the New South Wales court said that an agreement between two parties about the way property should be divided if the relationship broke up was legal. However, its legality was peculiar to it; the court did not say that any agreement made between de facto partners would be legal. The court said:

> The extent to which the court machinery can operate in this field can only be gradually tested as concrete cases appear. The courts should not become alchemists transmuting the ashes of dead passion into gold ... What this case does prove is that extra marital agreements are not for the amateur lawyer.

Thus, no hard and fast rules can be laid down to cover living together agreements. Every case is looked at on its merits by the courts. Contracts will be closely scrutinised, and their legality will depend on the talents of the lawyers drawing them up. Beware those who consult a lawyer whose talents are not recognised by the courts; and beware those who don't see the need for consulting a lawyer!

For young women intending to enter into relationships with others, current laws are not designed to make those relationships equal. The problems are not isolated to male-female relationships, but also arise in the case of lesbian, or communal relationships. Emel Corley favours living communally with other women, and sometimes with women and children. Sarah Gillman recognises the need for social understanding that monogamy is not conducive to ultimate happiness: "People need love from many others to fulfil themselves as individuals. No one person can bring out all characteristics in another." She continues:

> Unfortunately, there is still a belief in our society that a woman's true happiness and fulfilment depend on finding a partner, preferably someone of a similar social background and age as herself — male, of course!

It is important to design laws so that the rights of those who live in intimate relationships are protected, whether they are living communally, with a person of the same sex, or with a person of the opposite sex. It is foolish of anyone to believe that they can escape the operation of laws simply by not marrying. Laws exist that regulate marriage, de facto relationships and homosexual relationships. It is necessary to ensure that these laws are fair in their words and in their application.

Laws can be designed to be fair. Upon marriage, laws should recognise that the parties are equals, and that however they organise their lives, both are contributing equally to the marriage, including making equal contribution to any property accumulated in the marriage. With de facto relationships, it is equally appropriate to design laws recognising the relationship as equal and contributions by the parties as equal. This would mean that throughout the marriage and the de facto relationship — including de facto relationships between persons of the same sex — both parties would have equal rights to the assets, and upon divorce or break-up of the relationship both parties would continue to have equal rights. In this way, property would be divided equally between the parties on marriage or relationship break-up.[22]

Once the property and income component of marriage and similar relationships is recognised, it is fair to assume that other aspects of these relationships will improve. The oppression of women in marriage and other intimate relationships is brought about as a result of economic inequalities between women and men, and political and social inequalities which have followed from this. (With lesbian relationships, the economic inequality is absent, as are social and political inequalities between the parties. However, there are important legal disabilities for lesbians which must be rectified.) With changes at an economic level, women will be in a more equal position, and men will be forced to acknowledge this. That acknowledgement should have important psychological and social effects, as well as the concrete effect of women being able to assert their legal right over property accumulated by joint efforts.

For women choosing to live in lesbian relationships it is necessary to outlaw discrimination on grounds of sexual preference. In some states,[23] legislation exists or is proposed to give those discriminated against in the delivery of services, goods, accommodation, employment and education the opportunity to complain through the court system and assert their right to be treated equally with heterosexuals. Of course, the right to be treated equally with heterosexual *women* is not enough. And these problems extend to women who choose not to live in any relationship, but to remain single and to live alone. That choice should be equally valid, and equally supported by the law.

Beyond legislative changes, however, changes of attitude are necessary. However fair and just laws appear, their operation can be subverted if courts, lawyers, and others involved in their application do not subscribe to the view that women and men are equal and have equal entitlements. Changing attitudes and behaviours is far more difficult than changing the law. And not only the attitudes of legal personnel have to change. All men must learn to recognise the right of women to participate equally at all levels of society. This includes the right of each woman to enter into a relationship with a man, should she so choose, assured that her autonomy will not thereby be encroached upon. This recognition must go beyond lip service. If men come to understand the bonuses resulting from the development of a world where girls and women exercise equal rights with boys and men, a society can be created where, in Karen Ermacora's words, "in all areas . . . everyone has a right to do anything he or she wants to, according to individual degrees of wisdom, ability, and enthusiasm, without infringing the rights of others".

Michele Trewick

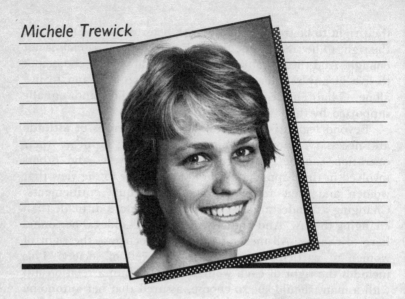

Michele Trewick *was born in Queensland in 1964. She was living with her parents in Cairns and studying to be a journalist at the time of writing.*

I was born nineteen years ago in Mount Isa, Queensland. My parents are both elderly, my father is retired. I am the second of two daughters — my sister is now married and has three children. I come from a working class Labor family in a working class suburb of Cairns, north Queensland.

When I was sixteen we had a "get to know each other" session at high school. We had to get a piece of paper and write our name, age, hobbies, interests and the person who most influenced our lives, and then pin it to our back for everyone to read. Although God and Jesus cropped up a couple of times, most girls wrote "my mother" as the person who had most influenced them. So did I. My mother is a dominant yet sensitive woman. She was forty-five when I was born, and although not an ardent feminist she has always instilled in me the belief that women are equal and that anything I wanted to do — I could — there was nothing or no one stopping me except myself. I often wonder where she got her equal attitudes from. She came from a small country town, survived a strict upbringing by Victorian parents, and married relatively early in life.

My parents have always encouraged me to get a good education, sometimes denied girls in financial crises; to get a good job; travel; and then if I wanted to, settle down. Personally, I don't think my parents would care if I never married — it was okay for my sister but I'm a different individual and I think they realise that. It suits my mother, I know, to stay at home and look after Dad, but that's not for me. Whether it is the experience of seeing my mother housebound for all these years, I don't know, but I'm going to hang on to my freedom for as long as is humanly possible.

While I feel my mother has been the most influential person in my life I can't forget my father. He has never treated me like the son he never had and I respect him for that. I feel that so many fathers like to get their daughters married and off their hands but my dad's different. Even though money was always limited my parents have always provided everything I needed for my education. They have never suggested, as others do, that education is a waste of time on a girl who will only grow up and get married and cease to need an education.

When I was younger, I thought that marriage was the most wonderful institution ever invented. And I still do, but in a different context. Marriage when I was fifteen represented security — someone to take care of me where my parents left off. Now marriage represents a union with someone I care for very much with both partners maintaining their independence. I get angry when I hear men complaining that marriage is a trap for them — and I think, my God, how selfish!

I doubt if many men would sacrifice the security and pleasure they get from their jobs to get married — yet it is these same men who expect their wives to stay at home and give up their working lives to look after their husbands. I believe that most men start to look down on their wives as mothers after a while instead of spouses and this I feel is a drastic mistake in any marriage. If my boyfriend asked me to marry him tomorrow I'd probably say yes. People think I'm crazy — here I am a strong advocate of women's rights and equality and yet given the chance I'd marry immediately. But if I did marry him, we'd still both maintain our jobs and thus our liberty. He would never ask me to give up my future career in journalism and I'd never ask him to give up his music. Why can't I have both — a career and a marriage? Why does it always boil down to a choice between the two? Feminism and marriage can be compatible or incompatible depending on the person. If you view marriage as a trap then it's unworkable — you might as well remain single. But if your husband understands your needs and rights then there should be no reason why they can't be combined. I will never cease to believe that both are right for me. Living together is useless. I regard a sense of permanency as integral to any relationship, and living together is, I feel, just two people who are afraid to make a lasting commitment.

As for children, I have and I always will believe that children are beautiful. My life would be incomplete without the birth of at least one child — this is the ultimate satisfaction of being a woman. I want to have as many children as is financially possible but I fully intend to return to work as soon as possible after the birth of my children. It's the quality of time you spend with your children, not the quantity. Fathers should play an equally active part in the rearing of children — not just the happy times but the wet nappies and the tantrums. Too often men want the pride of having children but are reluctant to accept the responsibility. Men and society as a whole have to throw away the traditional view that a child's place is with its mother and learn to take a greater part in the rearing and the teaching of children. I want to teach my sons to treat women with the respect they deserve.

When I read or hear about what some men say about women I wonder what kinds of mothers these people had. Why do some mothers believe that they have to raise their sons to be macho and manly? The greatest quality a woman can instil in her son is sensitivity. I also believe that a child needs both a mother and a father. Men haven't learnt to treat women equally yet but at the same time they do have an important place in parenting. I don't think I'd consider being a single parent — I feel I'd be denying something to my child. But this is just my personal view. Many children who have solely a mother often grow up with a greater sense of humanity and love than those emerging from a two-parent situation.

My choice of career is based only on my own decisions. I think my parents would have liked me to become a primary school teacher, which is a nice, feminine and ladylike profession. But while I adore children I have no wish to be an educator. I still feel that parents, teachers and career guidance officers are directly influencing girls to enter traditionally "female" domains such as nursing, teaching and secretarial studies. Society feels that a woman who wants to become, say, a mechanic, an engineer or an electrician is just trying to prove a point, demonstrating that she is trying to be equal or superior to a man. No one imagines that she might be interested, so she is either ridiculed or ignored. I guess it is the same for a man entering a generally female profession.

Only when fifty per cent of all people in all occupations are women can we truly say that we have a genuinely representative and democratic nation. Otherwise we are pushing women back into domestic tradition and not utilising the special and unique talents and qualities they possess to society's ultimate advantage. I don't really think journalism is a totally male-oriented career. Although they are still very limited, the numbers of female journos are increasing. And not just in women's magazines but also in hard-news newspapers and in television's current affairs shows. It's unfortunate but most women still have to work harder to maintain jobs whereas a male would only have to work half as hard.

I don't exactly dislike the term "feminist" but I believe it conjures up radical and "burn your bra" connotations. I prefer the term "equal opportunities" because it implies seeking equal rights and opportunities, and that is what women need. There was not any one moment in my life when I suddenly realised that I was a feminist. I have always believed that women are too often treated as second-class citizens and that this situation must be remedied immediately.

I'm hoping that there will come a day when a woman in a high position in a company won't be reported as an unusual phenomenon or a multi-talented superwoman, but a woman in an influential position will simply be nothing out of the ordinary and will be completely ignored by the media. Even with the degree of equality women have fought for already, when a newspaper or a magazine reports on a woman she is always described as "such and such, mother of three . . ." whereas in an equivalent report on a man it is never mentioned how many children he has sired. Whether this is deliberate discrimination or "paper policy" is inconsequential. It implies that children are a woman's responsibility rather than a man's,

and places her maternal role above her professional one.
Society must stop looking at women as wives and mothers, and,
rather, see them as individuals with a career future and as
potential breadwinners. With a universally accepted attitude
that women can work, perhaps traditional roles will be
interchanged and men will become house-husbands. But
society will have to change radically before this situation is
accepted.

Women can play a vital role in the equality of future
generations because of the profound influence mothers have
on their children's views and how they can structure their sons'
views on equality. Slowly feminism is changing our perceptions
of a woman's role in our society. Women are forging ahead in
areas that have previously been barred to them. Women
particularly have made strong inroads into politics and this is
the area in which significant development can come about. I
particularly admire the Australian Labor Party's Senator
Susan Ryan. She has distinctly feminist views but yet manages
to appear feminine. I also applaud Senator Janine Haines who
was number one on the Democrats' upper house ballot in South
Australia. She has earned the respect of her male colleagues
and that should be the ultimate goal of a woman seeking
equality and freedom of opportunity. Today the only way a
woman can hope to be taken seriously and equally is to get and
maintain the respect of the men with whom she works and who
share her life. You can't simply barge in and demand to be
treated equally. You have to achieve it. There is no overnight
solution to gender inequality — but sometimes I wonder how
many more years women must fight to achieve that which is
rightfully theirs. In our so-called civilised world there are still
some countries where women are denied the basic right to vote.

It would be hypocritical of me to favour equal rights for
women and yet deny them to other classes equally downtrodden. When I was younger I realised how discriminated against
women and blacks were. I thought how the odds of equality
would be stacked against you if you were an Aboriginal
woman. Thus I feel these women deserve special attention.
Aborigines and ethnic women are still locked within the cells of
tradition that women of English descent were able to break free
from years ago. Marriages are still arranged and there is still a
strong, inflexible patriarch at the head of many families.

Because they have limited educational and career opportunities, these women will have an even harder time trying to achieve equality.

If women were born the physically dominant sex, which is the only thing which keeps men superior (if intelligence and compassion were an assurance of dominance, then men would come in a very poor second), then this world would be void of war, violence and cruelty. It's a sad reflection on the physical domination of the world that the incidence of sexually related crimes, particularly against women, is increasing. It seems to be bred into males that it is their inalienable right to take sex when and where they like. Once men learn to respect women as equals, then the number of rapes and other crimes against women will decline.

Women have a sense of humanity, love and sensitivity that cannot be found in the majority of males. Women have a special concern for peace. This is why so many women are involved in the nuclear disarmament movement. Sometimes it seems that men have a natural desire for war — in order to prove their masculinity. Women have been endowed with a restful, conciliatory nature which makes them excellent leaders. Because of sexual oppression, women tend to strive for higher, often unattainable goals.

Peace is my major goal. Although I think the arms race must go on, in its own crude way being essential for keeping the peace, I continue to hope for disarmament and universal detente. This is basically a part of my feminist view because it is my belief that peace can only finally be achieved by women.

I believe that in the future women will progressively take on an increased and more important role in the world's decision-making. The 1983 Labor Party win in the federal election was a triumph not only for Bob Hawke as leader, but also for women politicians. Labor proved it wasn't afraid to put women in marginal seats. Hopefully, in the years to come women will command greater respect in the community and present inequalities will be eradicated or at least lessened. I hope that in the future, in some small way I will be able to make a contribution to the advancement and equality of women.

Karen Ermacora

Karen Ermacora, *born in Perth,
Western Australia in 1962, was
living in Melbourne when she
wrote her contribution and
studying at the Royal Melbourne
College of Art.*

At first, thinking about "growing up feminist" took me a little aback. In the past, I have not thought about whether I am a "feminist" or not. I haven't really understood the exact meaning of "feminism". Images coming to mind at first were those of angry women protesting against male dominance in society. But are those images a fuzzy reflection of ignorance and stereotyped perceptions?

Recently, the radio station I listen to reported on various people's ideas of the word "feminism". It seemed I am not the only one to be confused. Some callers were uncertain, some offered a wide range of meanings, including "a lady", "someone perfumed, with wafty clothes", "classy and able to hold her own", "intelligent, independent", "womanly". Clearly, although progressing strongly, the women's movement (or "feminism") does not have a single clear message in the general public's eyes. Does this mean that this group of women has not cried out loudly enough, or that people in general are not willing to listen? No doubt true feminists or anti-feminists could give their definite views of feminism's progress, whilst ignorance or confusion seem to hold sway elsewhere. That this is so limits the choices people can make. If the understanding of feminism is uncertain, then there are bound to be life avenues which are not explored by many people, out of sheer ignorance.

One of the steps in my understanding came when I sought a meaning for the word which I could relate to. So it was off to the *Collins English Dictionary*: "feminism — the doctrine that maintains the equality of the sexes." Equality! I believe in equality. Could I then consider myself a feminist?

My awareness of the feminist movement has only been quite recent and even then it has only trickled into my consciousness. Being at school means one has a narrow view of the world; leaving school usually widens the horizons. For me, my move from Perth to Melbourne after leaving school changed my environment and helped in the broadening. Here I encountered my first "feminist", who is a very dear friend of my father. Both she and my father have provided living and accessible examples of an independent lifestyle. They are intelligent and vibrant people who successfully support themselves and each other in all ways. It is through them and some of their friends that I have seen the possibility of alternative lifestyles. Not only is this way of living a reality for many people today, but it has definite advantages.

Living independently forces a degree of personal growth. On a practical level people have to learn new skills to do some jobs they have never before tackled. Because someone else is not going to provide a cushion against the world, the quality of a person's life is up to him or herself. Being free to take up any options that are of interest, people can be more intensely involved with the world on many levels. Motivated, stimulated, and alive, the individual is more able to develop a sense of confidence, personal worth, and wider aspirations.

Yet this freedom brings with it more questions. Do all women who believe in feminism have to remain separate from companions to fulfil their ideas? Is equality possible between women and men when they don't live closely together? Is it possible if they *do* live closely together? Equality should be one of the most important aspects in the lives of two people who have chosen to be together. As two individuals they will live, experience and grow, yet share the happenings of each other's lives. Existence could be quite separate in practical matters like finance, or could be combined so long as there is an awareness and understanding of the need for equality of both parties. The dependency which has developed in many stereotyped relationships has occurred because the partners have unthinkingly followed accepted tradition.

To me, a traditional "marriage" is acceptable only if people are making knowledgeable choices. I am reluctant to use the word marriage, because it seems to me to have neatly evened edges, allowing it to be easily slotted into a box. Unfortunately many people follow this road because they see it as the only possibility. Regardless of how they feel, they believe they must quash certain facets of their personality. Desperate attempts are made to comply with expectations so they can receive acceptance. With this perspective, those who believe they have "failed" often feel dismal and worthless. They classify themselves as useless, feeling that "life" is irretrievably lost.

When people discover their own feelings and needs, and are not ashamed to acknowledge them, then more satisfaction and happiness follow. Society has such strong chains, built up over centuries, that it is difficult to escape them. But growing up with adults who are freer in their thinking, and who do not blindly follow traditions simply because they are there, has helped me to listen to my internal self. This gives me a greater chance of happiness and a sense of complete living.

Equality between people should not mean "sameness". It should mean "the same value". Each person, though different in many ways, is important. Realistically, a certain amount of social acceptance is usually necessary, but it should be possible to escape the fear of having to conform to set rules. My family life has taught me to tolerate other people's choices. Their choices may not always be understood, but should be at least accepted. Today, so many relationships are laughed at or abused simply because they are different from what everyone "expects".

In my learning about equality, for me there are many areas in which the word holds much meaning. I give a lot of weight to the specific theme of decisions about marriage and relationships, because these tend to greatly influence other areas of people's lives and sometimes might overshadow them completely. In all areas, marriage, work, home life, school, vacation life — everyone has a right to do anything he or she wants to, according to individual degrees of wisdom, ability, and enthusiasm, without infringing the rights of others.

I want to live in a world where the right to do anything is a reality. If all work and leisure activities were available to us all, natural selection would sort things out. A person with little strength would not be able to take on a job requiring mammoth muscle power. A person with a low mental capacity would not be able to take on a job demanding a high intellectual standard. But both jobs and both persons are equally valuable and valid, and this would be recognised. In such a world it would also be remembered that mental, physical and spiritual (why are there so few female priests?) abilities overlap within the sexes and vary with individuals. Little is black and white; rather there are many shades of grey. So, if every possibility was a real option, many more people would feel satisfied with their lives.

The welfare of children is ultimately the responsibility of both parents. Discussions about having children should not be light-hearted. Such plans should be scrutinised seriously. After all, the children of today are the adults of tomorrow (they will be deciding your pension rate!) and although you may not be around, the future of the world is at stake. Without children, human beings would not develop and broaden their minds; love and discovery would not be as sweet. So take care!

The duties of both parents are clear. Although the woman carries the unborn child, the original rights and duties go further back to the time of conception. An equal contribution from both parents creates the child. The child is therefore the responsibility of both parents from time of conception. Decisions must be jointly agreed to even if they determine one parent only should take care of the child.

But what of myself, my future, my relationship to feminism? This remains unresolved for me.My future aspirations and directions are not yet decided, and I do not know whether they will centre on feminist ideals. I prefer to live and explore rather than plan. There are many feminist issues of which I am not yet fully aware. Probably with time these will become clearer to me. Yet I do believe in equality and the equal value of each person. I know this belief will be part of the future me.

CHAPTER FOUR

Children

Man from Nebraska: "Don't you think that the best thing a woman can do is to perform well her part in the role of wife and mother? My wife has presented me with eight beautiful children: is not this a better life work than that of exercising the right of suffrage?"

Elizabeth Cady Stanton: "I have met few men, in my life, worth repeating eight times."

Elizabeth Cady Stanton,
Eighty Years and More, 1898

No woman can call herself free who does not own and control her body. No woman can call herself free until she can choose consciously whether she will or will not be a mother.

Margaret Sanger,
Woman and the New Race, 1920

That the child is the supreme aim of woman is a statement having precisely the value of an advertising slogan.

Simone de Beauvoir,
The Second Sex, 1952

The only thing that seems eternal and natural in motherhood is ambivalence.

Jane Lazarre,
The Mother Knot, 1978

The purpose of marriage is motherhood. This litany has been repeated through the years. There is no suggestion that man's purpose in life is marriage and fatherhood; he is given latitude in his ambitions, career and lifestyle. Why the difference? The basis of women's role has been summed up by Freud in his (in)famous statement: "Biology is destiny." For women, biologically programmed to bear children, dominant thought decrees that the child-bearing function *should* be exercised. Of course, this ignores the fact that some women, because of infertility or other health reasons that prevent them from conceiving or from bearing children, are not able to fulfil their alleged destiny, at least by natural means. It also ignores the fact that some women do not wish to have children, and that women who do, do not generally find total fulfilment for life from the process.

Today, the inability of a woman to have a child is perceived to be a problem. Thousands of dollars are spent on in-vitro fertilisation programmes. Women attend medical clinics for extended courses of treatment, hoping to gain or regain the ability to become pregnant. Adoptive mothers undertake hormonal treatment in an effort to breastfeed their adoptive babies. Women making the choice not to have children are frequently faced with charges that they are selfish or unnatural. Those having children but wishing to continue their careers, or simply to leave their young children in childcare whilst taking some time to themselves are regarded as placing their offspring's emotional wellbeing in jeopardy. Yet the world has not always been thus. Past attitudes and realities are important for understanding today's motherhood debate. They are part-icularly important to young women (and young men) faced with choices about their futures.

When patriarchy gained control over sexual relationships, the production of children was dictated as a purpose for marriage. This came about with changes in economic organis-ation, as children were necessary for property and labouring reasons. Economic demands meant children were essential for the passing down of property and consolidation of family fortunes. Without male heirs, the blood strain would die out (female children were not regarded as heirs, nor as trans-mitting the family blood line). For serfs, children were an absolute requirement: more workers made the lord of the manor better able to expand his landholdings and increase his crop production. This might improve the lot of his workers. With the growth of the free working class, children were important for survival. In a society where wages-for-work formed the basis of living, the more children in the family, the more money coming in. Very young children — often two, three, four years of age — were shunted off into the coal mines and factories, or put out to work in the fields. Before the industrial revolution, they worked in the home at spinning or similar tasks. With the growing power of the church, children became the religious as well as the economic reason for marriage. Sexual intercourse was regarded as wrong in itself. Whatever individuals might privately think, the pure abstained from sexual relations and joined the church; those who were not so "strong" married and put their energies into reproducing themselves.[1]

Yet bearing children predated, by thousands of years, formalised marriage as we know it. Sexual relationships between members of different clans were established to create friendly relations between those clans. The aim was to give pleasure and to prevent, as far as possible, antagonism between members of opposing tribes. Strict taboos prevented women and men (in theory at least) from the same clan engaging in sexual intercourse together, which meant it was necessary to seek partners from outside the group. Members of pre-literate societies had no conception of the way in which children are biologically produced. Many believed that women became pregnant through eating particular foods. They did not see sexual intercourse and pregnancy as related. Even when biological fact was made known to tribal communities, they did not believe it. A male anthropologist working amongst Pacific Islanders records:

> Their attitude to their own children ... bears witness to their ignorance of any causal relation between congress and the ensuing pregnancy. A man whose wife has conceived during his absence will cheerfully accept the fact and the child, and he will see no reason at all for suspecting her of adultery. One of my informants told me that after over a year's absence he returned to find a newly born child at home. He volunteered this statement as an illustration and final proof of the truth that sexual intercourse has nothing to do with conception ...
>
> My friend Layseta, a great sailor and magician of Sinaketa, spent a long time in his later youth in the Amphilett Islands. On his return he found two children, borne by his wife during his absence. He is very fond of them and of his wife; and when I discussed the matter with others, suggesting that one of these children could not be his, my interlocutors did not understand what I meant.[2]

Because there was no realisation amongst pre-literate peoples that men had a biological connection to the children they sired, fathers had no rights and no special relationship with them. Motherhood was a concept known to these societies and it was between women and children that ties were strongest. However, *all* adult women in the clan played an important role in children's lives: often babies were passed from woman to woman and suckled by any, or all of them. Ties between brothers and sisters were strong. A son's status was determined not by the status of his biological father, but by the matriclan into which he was born. He "belonged" to the matriclan of his mother (her tribal group of women and men) and this determined his place in society.

The realisation that children were biologically produced played a significant role in justifying the father's control over his children, and his right to bind them to him in order to pass down his inheritance. Children were important in maintaining social order. An heir of the aristocracy carried on his father's line; a tradesman's son carried on his father's trade; the son of a serf remained a serf; a working class father had a right to the labour of his children. The need for men to establish father-hood rights was important to their immortality:

> . . . a man is immortal only if he has a son. This belief has become modified both in language and ideas, but is still general, even among ourselves; a man wishes for a son to bury him and look after his grave; to keep his memory green; to succeed to his name or his title, and so keep it alive; to keep up the old place and the old family portraits. The Roman nobles kept their ancestors alive by means of portrait statues, and these bring us back to Egypt, and the portrait statues which were associated with mummification.[3]

During the Victorian era sons were obliged to live up to the standards set for them by their fathers. The relationship between father and son was generally not that of the caring, loving, kindly patriarch. Even if caring appeared to exist from father to son, behind this lay the real power of patriarchal authority. This is well illustrated in a letter written from father to son on 18 September 1866:

> James,
>   As your unblushing impudence and undutiful conduct to me of late and your total disregard for the domestic happiness of myself, your mother, yourself and your brothers

and sisters render it painfully distasteful to me at present to hold any personal conversation with you, I have thought it only my duty as your Father to give my commands to you in writing, in order that you may not mistake that which you will have strictly to observe if you have any wish or desire to continue one of my household.

1st. You will have to get up every morning and clean the knives and forks which may be in daily use in our house.

2nd. Get yourself ready for your daily employment and be at your work in proper time according to office hours.

3rd. To stop quarrelling and bickering with your brothers and sisters.

4th. To be at home evenings not later than half past nine o'clock and lastly though not least, to attend divine worship every Sunday *twice*.

I am compelled to adopt these rules from the simple fact that you appear to have forgotten the 5th commandment and abandoned all idea of studying to improve your mind or future position in life, and taken up an empty notion of pride and indolence.

A violation of any *one* of the aforesaid rules or even an omission of them without a *satisfactory reason* will render it imperative on my part to forbid your longer remaining sheltered under my roof, in which case I hope and trust you will provide yourself with a better home.

Yours.

(Sgd) Wm. Orchard.[4]

By this time, mothers had lost any rights over their children, and their relationship was maintained because mother and children lived in the husband/father's household. Under the law, custodial rights resided in the father alone. For any court to interfere with "father right" was unusual, and the character and actions of a father had to meet a high standard of dastardly behaviour for him to lose custody. Even then, the mother did not automatically gain custody. Indeed, for many years she had no rights at all. Equity courts tempered this somewhat, eventually granting the mother a right to plead for custody in those few cases where it was held that the father was grossly incompetent and unsuited as the children's guardian.

Even then, the mother had no greater right to custody than any other family member, or even strangers. If a woman left her husband's house because he was cruel to her, threatened her life, or for any other reason, she had no rights in respect of her children.

Tragically, women were often unaware of the law until too late. Lady Caroline Norton was unhappy with her cruel and alcoholic husband, and fled from his home hoping her children would follow her when she reached her family. Her husband sued her for divorce on the ground that she had committed adultery with a close friend, Lord Melbourne. The charge was found by a jury to be entirely false. Following the trial, Caroline Norton sought a divorce "by reason of cruelty", laying before her lawyers "the many instances of violence, injustice, and ill-usage, of which the trial [on adultery charges] was but the crowning example".[5] She was told she had condoned the cruelty by returning to her husband's house to take care of the children. Agitating for changes to the law, she wrote:

> I learnt, too, the *Law* as to my children — that the right was with the father; that neither my innocence or his guilt could alter it; that not even his giving them into the hands of a mistress, would give me any claim to their custody. The eldest was but six years old, the second four, the youngest two and a half, when we were parted. I wrote, therefore, and petitioned the *father and husband*, in whose power I was, for leave to see them — for leave to keep them, till they were a little older. Mr Norton's answer was, that I should not have them; that if I wanted to see them, I might have an interview with them at the chambers of his attorney. I refused, and wrote as follows to my solicitor, who had conveyed his decision to me:
>
> "However bitter it may be to me, I must decline seeing my children in the manner proposed. I say nothing of the harshness, the inhumanity of telling me I must either see them at the chambers of his solicitor, or not at all; but I say it is not *decent* that the father of those children should force me, their mother, out of the very tenderness I bear them, to visit them in the chambers of the attorney who collected the evidence, examined the witnesses, and conducted the proceedings for the intended divorce [on grounds of adultery

with Lord Melbourne]. I say it is not decent — nay, that even if I were guilty, it would not be decent to make me such a proposal. But I am innocent. I have been pronounced innocent by a jury of my countrymen . . . Why, then, are my children kept from me? — from me whom even their own witnesses proved to be a careful and devoted mother? Mr Norton says, the Law gives him my children . . ."

Eventually, Caroline Norton was permitted to have the children visit her at her brother's house. But Mr Norton expressly limited the time of their stay "to one half-hour, sending them with two of the women who had been witnesses on the trial, who stated that their 'orders' were to remain in the room . . .". She wrote: "I was not allowed even to see my baby of two years old without these '*witnesses*'."

The "maternal instinct"

Despite the very real grief of Caroline Norton in her struggle to secure her children's companionship, it is wrong to suppose that motherhood as depicted today — the loving woman doting tirelessly on her brood — has been eternal and universal. From the middle ages until the late nineteenth century women produced numerous offspring. Many died in infancy. Many died, together with their mothers, during childbirth. A number of children born to one husband and wife might be called "Charles" or "Charlotte" or some other name traditional within the family, so that if one died the name would nevertheless continue. Some mothers breastfed their babies, but it was certainly not the "proper" or only accepted method. Mothers of children born into high society had their children breastfed — but not often by themselves. According to Elizabeth Badinter, writing in *The Myth of the Maternal Instinct*, in 1780 over 21,000 babies were born in Paris, but of these only a thousand were breastfed by the natural mother; another thousand were sent to a wet nurse (the infant mortality rate was 26.5 per cent).[6] In England the aristocracy adopted the practice of having live-in wet nurses; those less well placed sent their children out to other women's houses for breastfeeding.

When children grew older, they were sent away from home to undertake live-in job training. In the upper echelons, children were sent away to court to act as ladies' maids or valets; some took their place at court as attendants to royalty. At lower levels children went into service in county homes as maids, bootboys or tweenies, progressing to butler, valet and first lady's maid. Others went into trade, serving as apprentices away from home. With the growth of commerce, many children lived in, learning the trade of haberdashery in department stores with living quarters overhead. They left home as young as eight and nine years old; some were even younger when they were "sold" into the business world. In Australia, as in England, children were sold into service, sent out to baby farms — where many died through lack of adequate care[7] — or were placed in the care of nannies so that their mothers could free themselves for other tasks or simply for being society ladies.

Some women may well have been forced by economic necessity to farm out their babies and apprentice their children, denying themselves a close relationship with them. Some may have been incapable of breastfeeding their own children, due to poor diet and bad health arising out of appalling living conditions. Nonetheless it is clear that some women at least did not look upon motherhood as an all-consuming task, requiring total dedication. As well, some women freed themselves from motherhood by committing infanticide, a not uncommon practice in England during the fifteenth, sixteenth and seventeenth centuries, and extending into later times when it was brought to Australia.[8] Babies were smothered, drowned, left in the open to die of cold or exposure and some had their throats cut. Children were abandoned in the streets, in doorways, in the vestries of churches, at charitable institutions. Not all mothers dealt with their children in this way because they did not care for infants or because they preferred not to have their lives disrupted by childcare and child-rearing as well as pregnancy and childbirth. Many women were constrained to do so by economic circumstances or censoriousness abounding in a society that deplored the evidence of illicit sexual activity. However, some women freely gave away their children because traditional mothering did not suit them.

Both financial hardship and women's unwillingness to become mothers (whatever their financial situation) are similarly revealed in reports on the decline in birthrate, which

occurred in Australia toward the end of the nineteenth
century. In 1903 the New South Wales government established
a Royal Commission ". . . to make full and diligent enquiry
into the causes which have contributed to the decline in the
birthrate of New South Wales, and the effects of the restriction
of childbearing upon the wellbeing of the community". The
New South Wales government was the first in the world to hold
any such investigation.[9] Witnesses coming before the
Commission reported upon "the readiness, and even the spont-
aneity, of married people in admitting a deliberate restriction
in the number of their children by taking recourse to artificial
checks . . .". The reason married couples gave was lack of
finances to pay for the upkeep of more children, but witnesses
and the Commission refused to accept this as the real reason in
many — perhaps the majority — of cases. Rather, they considered the majority of women sought contraception because
they were unwilling to submit to the strain and worry of
mothering. This same majority, said the Commission, had a
dislike of the "interference with pleasure and comfort"
involved in childbearing and child-rearing. Women desired "to
avoid the actual physical discomfort of gestation, parturition,
and lactation". Furthermore, they suffered from a "love of
luxury and of social pleasures". This sybaritic approach to life
was increasing, the Commission intoned:

> A circumstance that causes grave misgivings as to the future
> is that so many women do not realise the wrong involved in
> the practices of prevention and abortion. They converse
> with one another upon these subjects apparently without
> shame, and freely approach doctors and chemists in order to
> procure the means to gratify their desires . . . [10]

In support, medical practitioners gave evidence of the
frequency with which women left country districts to travel to
the metropolis seeking abortions. Pharmacists and doctors
from Pambula to Newcastle commented that women were
more ready to discuss abortion and came often to them seeking
help: "I remember a woman coming and asking me, and I said
I did not do that sort of thing; and she said, 'Oh, it would be
just as well; I have been down twice before to Sydney, but if
you do it for me it would not cost so much'."
    In 1929 the Australian government commissioned a report
on maternal and child welfare in Australia. Again, extensive

comment was made upon the voluntary limitation of families leading to a decline in the birthrate. In 1944 the National Health and Medical Research Council produced a report lamenting declining birthrates, which it saw as mainly due to financial and other stresses. So serious was the situation in the Council's eyes that it deemed it necessary to call for comment from as many women as possible to discover why they voluntarily limited their families. The call was given wide publicity by the daily press and radio broadcast:

> . . . the Council wishes to make an appeal to women. Those who have deliberately resolved not to have children, or to limit their families, must have had some reason. On the economic, or other social reasons, the Council can have, at best, only secondhand evidence. The Council would like to know from the women themselves what their reasons have been . . . [11]

As soon as the invitation appeared, "replies began to come in freely". In the first seven days 680 replies were received by the Council. The final total was 1400 replies.

Commissions and reports have done nothing to assuage the concern of some about the current Australian birthrate. Concern has been voiced at regular intervals about the "failure" of women to produce the requisite number of children. As late as 1980 the then federal Minister of Health, Michael MacKellar, was calling for women to cease paid employment and start having babies. Women did not heed the call. It cannot be doubted that women do not always choose to bear children, and that as far as they are able (by use of contraceptives, abortion, and fending off husbands demanding their "rights"), they plan the number of children they will bear. According to the evidence, many — if not most — women seek to limit the number of children to which they give birth. In 1974, of a working class sample of women expecting their first babies, two-thirds of the pregnancies were unplanned and half were not wanted. They were classed as mistakes, resulting from the failure of birth control methods.[12]

Studies have found that before or upon marriage women generally plan to have more children than they will later decide to have. After five or six years of marriage a decrease in desired family size is recorded. In *How Women See Themselves*, Faye Fransella and Kay Frost attribute this to "post-nuptial optimism ... evaporating with the experience of childbearing".[13] Some women increase their expectations of family size after marriage; some have more children than they originally planned and are satisfied. Whatever the case, it is clear that women are not simply programmed to have babies. Rather, many make decisive choices about childbearing; of those who do not, or who are precluded from the choice, many are unhappy at having "mistakes".

Current childbearing debates

Today, research shows that girls and boys desire to marry in the future in order to procreate. British children express a wish to have children as a strong reason for marrying, although more girls than boys say this. Swedish, Norwegian and Danish children have similar views.[14] Upon reaching adulthood, however, children and marriage do not necessarily go hand in hand. Diana Forward says she wants to have children and bring them up herself. Fiona Giles would like to have children, but not within a nuclear family as she does not see it as a positive means of organising society. Sarah Gillman expresses the view that single parenting is a positive lifestyle, but noted that marriage is usually seen as a first step to raising a family. On the other hand, Cathy Henry would like her own children and prefers the nuclear family to other alternatives.

In Australia, not all births are within marriage. The proportion of ex-nuptial births increased in 1977 to a little more than ten per cent, up from an average of eight per cent of all births in the period 1966 to 1970. Figures show that:

> ... while the proportion of all births that are ex-nuptial has increased, the actual number of ex-nuptial births has declined; and because there are now more unmarried women capable of having them [because the age at which women and men marry has risen in recent years], this means that the rate has declined too. It has declined especially among teenagers. The 15-19 year age group still bears most of the ex-nuptial births, but the rate of such births among women this age has shown a marked decline.[15]

During the period 1972 to 1977, the number of children born to girls between the ages of fifteen and nineteen years declined by seventeen per cent. At the same time the number of births to married women between the same ages declined by almost half — forty-two per cent. There is a decline in fertility among the youngest age group of women, married or unmarried, and "the biggest percentage decline turns out to be among those who are married".

Recent evidence suggests that although as girls they might express a desire to marry and have children, when the time comes many women — up to fifty per cent — are not so ready to accept the traditional role. More and more people "are considering what it means to become a parent before they decide whether or not to have children".[16] As Mary Gartrell writes, "I don't want to have children and see marriage (still) going hand in hand with having them. Not wanting children, I don't see the point of getting married." She continues:

Although I love children and have had lots of experience looking after them, at all ages, I would rather they weren't mine. I cannot see myself being able to bring up children as well and as carefully as my mother and father, yet have an interesting and exciting career.

Emel Corley says that she enjoys being with other women and children and sometimes thinks that she might have her own children, but it is not important to her. Anna Donald expresses the "child-free" situation as one where a person chooses to be a parent because she wants to, not as one where she refuses to be a parent.

Today women (and men) are open about their desire not to parent, whether or not they are married. One woman is reported as saying:

It's too bad that young women think that they have to have children in order to be "fulfilled". I'm fifty-six, never had kids, and feel as "fulfilled" as I could possibly be. Our lives can be rich with work, friends, other people's children and many other things. I don't think that motherhood is the right choice for every woman.[17]

Nancy Romer concludes that people who choose not to bear their own children "believe their needs for achievement, influence, immortality, excitement, and loving relationships can be met through other personal relationships; careers; and work in the community":

Those who choose not to have children do not necessarily dislike children. Some people who are particularly interested in children, such as teachers, prefer not to be with children at home as well as at work; they may desire to have close relationships with many children over the years and spend more free time with other adults or by themselves.[18]

MacIntyre comments that sex, marriage and childbearing should not be seen as inextricably linked, as has been the case in popular thought and research to date; rather, their independence of each other should be recognised:

Though sex, marriage and reproduction may be linked empirically in a particular society and its dominant ideology, we still need to enquire into the processes leading to them and the meanings attributed to them. We cannot assume *a priori* that people have babies because they are married, or marry in order to have babies; nor that people have babies because they have had sex, or that they have sex in order to produce babies.[19]

Although some couples believe their lives would be lonely, empty and boring without children (and this begs the question of whether both parties in fact agree, or whether one or the other has differing thoughts), Jessie Bernard's research shows children do not make marriages, nor women, happier, either initially or when older. Women married with children were more likely to find marriage restrictive than were married women without children. In one study the most frequent response by married women to the question "how is a woman's life changed by having children?" was that children restricted women's freedom. Not more than half were positive about the changes that bearing children bring to women's lives. Women with children were less satisfied with their relationship with their husbands and described themselves as having marital problems. Women without children had the highest levels of satisfaction about marriage and those with small children had the lowest levels; those whose children had grown up and left home recorded higher levels of satisfaction, more nearly reaching the satisfaction levels of women who had not borne children.[20]

Of course, these findings do not reveal that the problem necessarily lies with the children. They may well indicate that the problem lies with the way our society is structured to deal with children. Anna Donald sees fathers who fail to contribute to childrearing as placing "an enormous load on the mother". Mary Gartrell says that in today's world, a woman has to make a choice between a career and children. This she considers unfair: "Because the mother bears the child should not mean that she has also to be the one who forgoes a career to rear the child." She regrets the current need for super-powers of women and men to achieve childrearing together with careers. This conjures up the image of the superwoman living a full life with children and career, that has little relationship to reality and places an unfair burden on women, not only causing them to try to fulfil the image, but destroying their self-confidence when life at such a pace becomes impossible. That any young women conclude they must be superwomen to have a career and children means they are being indoctrinated into beliefs that will ultimately be destructive of them.

The responsibility young women feel for the children they may have, or other children for whom they may care, is evident in Diana Forward's comments. She feels strongly that taking a decision about childbearing means that a woman has to ensure they have the opportunity of a good lifestyle. This might make women postpone a career until "after [the] children have become a little independent".

Discrimination in parenting

The emphasis on woman's role as major childcarer, totally responsible for the children until they began school, and in many cases retaining responsibility until the children turned eighteen or twenty-one was a development which was given an impetus by the work of John Bowlby during the late 1940s and 1950s. It was hurried along by research which set out to show maternal deprivation as the root of most social ills. Lack of a mother's constant care during the first six months after birth would inevitably lead to delinquency, psychopathy and any other personality disorders, the pundits intoned. "Latch key children", those left by mothers to mind themselves during the day or after school while the mothers were in paid employment, would develop poorly and be likely to follow antisocial or even criminal paths.[21]

Yet these views had little relationship to reality. More, they were deliberately promulgated to ensure that women took up with a vengeance their mothering role, following the greater freedom they had enjoyed as paid workers in non-traditional fields during the war, in the absence of men. An idealised picture of motherhood was created, resulting in women suffering a certain schizophrenia through the disparity between the "ideal" and the reality. Having children and being involved in their upbringing is enjoyed by many women — but at the same time they are confronted with numerous disabilities arising directly out of their motherhood status. Those who wish women to continue fulltime in this role in fact support a system which operates to drive women out of it: the fulltime role would be enhanced rather than reduced in attraction if women were not required to take full responsibility for child-rearing and childcare. Furthermore, mothers' involvement with their children would be of greater quality if women did not have to confirm to themselves that their mothering role is all-important. As Faye Fransella and Kay Frost point out in *How Women See Themselves*, the conventional motherhood message leads some women to ". . . expect that when they have children they will want to devote their time to them, to the exclusion of everything else. Actual experience of children dampens their idealism and work becomes more attractive as a result . . .".[22]

Middle age affects women diversely. Some women feel empty and lost without their motherhood role, the children having grown up and departed. A fifty-one-year-old home-maker described herself as lacking any independent identity:

> I'm Dennis and Derek Clark's mother, and Mike Clark's wife. That's who I am, right there. After that, I'm just a blank. I don't know if I'm anything else; it's been so many years . . .[23]

Other women feel freed when their children attain adulthood and branch out into new pursuits. They regret their children's going not at all. Typically, little research has been done on men's reactions to the traditional version of fatherhood, although in middle age men are reported as saying they regret the lack of communication they have with their children. They frequently see this as resulting from lack of interaction with the children at a young age, due to work pressures and role demands. In one study men were most upset by their children's departure; they felt ". . . the years had slipped by without their really getting to know their children . . . Many fathers want to hold on to their children at this point". Mothers in the study believed they had played a significant part in each step of their children's development and separation from them was easily adjusted to as being "right".[24]

In talking about her desire to have children, Michele Trewick says she believes that fathers should take an equally active part in child-rearing, "not just the happy times but the wet nappies and the tantrums". Karen Ermacora similarly states that the welfare of children should be the responsibility of both parents. Mary Gartrell says both parents should make an equal contribution to decisions about the raising and care of children. Other contributors talk about the need for positive, adequate childcare provisions outside the home. Yet despite government commitments in the 1980s and real efforts to expand grants to childcare centres, providing moneys on an even-handed basis, childcare remains an inadequately fulfilled need in Australia. As well, childcare expenses cannot be claimed as tax deductions, except for a limited number of three- to five-year-olds in "educational establishments" where claims can be made for educational expenses up to $250. Differences in approach have led to a debate developing around the question of childcare expenses and their rebate.[25] Whatever the outcome, it is clear that until childcare is made readily accessible to all, women will continue to bear the greater burden of responsibility for children's comfort and everyday care.

Even where men are involved in caring for their own children, it appears from research that they are more likely to concern themselves with the "good times" — the playtimes, going out, reading to happy children at night, and the like. The less happy times — of dirty nappies, squalling faces and general naughtiness — are more often the realm of mothers. Graeme Russell's research in *The Changing Role of Fathers?* shows that although men may perform a goodly number of childcaring tasks in a relatively small number of cases, their performance is generally limited to the more appealing portions of the work.[26]

Financing children is expensive. In many cases the cost of childcare is borne solely by the mother. When she determines to re-enter the paid workforce, her husband "allows" her to do so, on the basis that she make arrangements for the children. Where a woman is separated or divorced from her husband and has custody of the children, her financial position will in most cases be far less secure than his. Now, under the *Family Law Act*, both women and men can be required to pay maintenance in respect of their children, where those children are in the custody of the other parent. This is eminently fair. Yet the problem is that where men are ordered to pay maintenance for child costs, they rarely comply with the order. A report released by the federal Attorney-General in February 1984 showed that some 74,000 Australians (mostly mothers) are receiving maintenance payments. It also shows that nearly two-thirds of recipients "receive less than $1500 each year in maintenance, and that they are much poorer than the rest of the community"; 77 per cent have a gross income annually of less than $10,000. The weekly cost of clothing and footwear, food, household provisions, heat, electricity and gas, toys and presents, pocket money, schooling and entertainments adds up to $21.20 for a five-year old and $27.90 for an eleven-year old. These costs exclude housing (mortgages, rents, rates, bonds, and the like), transport, school fees, school uniforms, childcare, holidays, and medical and dental expenses.[27] The figures are for *a basic survival costing*. Women, having the lowest incomes, the least opportunities of holding jobs where flexibility is possible (so that they have time off for children's illnesses, visiting their schools, and so on), and the least possibility of employing a live-in housekeeper and childcarer, nonetheless are expected to take the major responsibility for children!

It is clear that men are prone to forget their responsibilities in respect of their children, particularly where those children are left in the mother's custody. Thus, the Attorney-General's report states:

> . . . a very large number of people are missing out on maintenance because their orders are not adequately enforced or because they have not been able to obtain an order in the first place. There are many more people than the 74,000 actually receiving maintenance who ought to be receiving it. This is a disturbing indictment of our present system.[28]

The people who are missing out on maintenance payments are, ultimately, the children for whom the money is ordered to be paid. Do their fathers not care for their welfare? The problem does not lie in the father's having no money to pay: maintenance awards are not made unless the person against whom an order is made is financially able to meet that order. Commenting on the recommendations in the Attorney-General's report, Neil states:

> . . . it's just as likely that a man in a sound financial position will renege on his responsibilities [as one less well-off]. If the person is determined to avoid maintenance payments there is little that can be done to force him . . . [Clerks] at the local Magistrates' court [are] usually part-time and [have] no legal powers of enforcement. They don't seem to get anywhere with the system and eventually . . . get tired of pushing and just drop out completely.
>
> The onus then falls on the custodial parent, usually the mother, to chase the reluctant payer through the courts at her own expense . . .
>
> Probably the worst offenders . . . are self-employed people, determined not to pay up. They are certainly the most difficult . . . to chase up . . .[29]

To improve the situation, a national collection agency was to be established to chase up payments and to make automatic wage deductions if a parent falls behind with payments by, say, thirty days. Ideally, it is suggested, deductions should be automatic, comparable with deductions for tax payments.

Discrimination can also arise where women choose to be mothers but choose also to live in a lesbian relationship. In discussing parenting abilities of lesbian mothers, Lois writes:

> There are, undoubtedly, special issues involved in lesbian parenting — some challenges are some advantages . . . . Callahan writes that a good parent basically protects and nurtures her child. Through providing this care, the parent enjoys, entices, and encourages the child into life. Simultaneously, the good parent withdraws and separates from the child so that it can become independent and grow . . .
> To ease such transitions throughout childhood, perhaps all children should have lesbian mothers: researchers comparing lesbians and heterosexual women have found that lesbians were more independent, resilient, reserved, self-sufficient and composed . . . and that they rated higher in self-confidence. . . . One who is self-aware and self-assured

would seem to be better able to nurture, care, and support while also letting go.

As in all families with children, lesbian mothers "worry when their children are sick and make endless peanut butter sandwiches . . .".[30]

Yet this is not the way courts usually regard lesbians in general and lesbian mothers in particular.

Bitter battles have been fought in the Family Court by women who are mothers and living in lesbian relationships, who wish to retain or to secure custody of their children following divorce. In *In the Marriage of N. and N.* a private enquiry agent was hired by the husband to track his ex-wife and secure evidence of her relationship with another woman. The trial judge awarded custody to the father. It was agreed by the Full Court on appeal that in the case:

> . . . there was a great deal of evidence given about the alleged lesbian relationship between the appellant and co-respondent. This is a matter for regret and it is regrettable also that in a case such as this an inquiry agent should have been involved to the extent he was . . . His Honour said that the mother's fitness was of serious concern because of this relationship . . .[31]

Delivering her judgement in the appeal, the Chief Judge of the Family Court commented on this, saying: "I, myself, would not put it as high as that." Yet the court does not always take the latter, less judgemental view. Nor is every litigant able to afford to appeal. It costs money which women do not come by as readily as men.

Furthermore, the question remains whether lesbianism has a negative effect on mothering. Many lesbians and others would consider it is not — but if it is, then this is not because lesbianism is wrong, but because society regards it as such and has developed attitudes which make living in such a relationship difficult. In *In the Marriage of Spry and Spry* this issue was crucial in determining that custody should be awarded to the father of two girls aged ten and six, with weekend access granted to the mother. The court said:

> It is my view that lesbianism per se does not make a mother unfit to have custody, but it is a factor which cannot be ignored and must be taken into account with the other

factors that make up the total situation. Of equal if not greater importance than the question of a child's sexual orientation in a homosexual milieu, is the question as to whether, in that milieu, they may become the subject of intolerance. Community attitudes towards homosexuality have, fortunately, changed over the recent years, but not ... to such a degree as to ensure that the children will have freedom from spiteful comment from their peer group who may be influenced by the attitudes of their parents. [Their mother] herself admitted that there could be problems from parents of her children's friends not permitting their children to visit the two little girls in an overtly lesbian household. I believe that [the women] have endeavoured to face up to these problems honestly and courageously but their passion for each other has, I believe, blunted their perceptions of the problems the children, if they are in their care and control, are likely to face in today's society.[32]

In *In the Marriage of Cartwright* the mother was sufficiently fortunate to gain custody — but at a price! The judge found comfort in the fact that in evidence the mother had said she would "do all she could to prevent the children finding out that she was a homosexual". She further said she did not think that she would like her children to become homosexuals. She said that homosexuality was in her view "an unfortunate thing". The judge went on:

> She said that if asked by [her daughter] about the matter, she would have to say that homosexuality was normal for some, but that she would not say it was bad, posing the rhetorical question as to how she could say this to her daughter when she was homosexual herself. She said that her daughter appeared to show normal heterosexual responses and outlook and had a boyfriend at school ...
> The wife is certainly no homosexual crusader ...[32]

Custody was awarded on the mother giving an undertaking that she would not "expose" the children to her homosexual proclivities: "In my opinion if the wife is prepared to give such an undertaking then the welfare of the children dictates that they should be in her custody ..." The undertaking was to the effect that:

> ... until further order of the court the wife would refrain

from any act or word which would reasonably be calculated to suggest to any of the children that she or any friend of hers is a lesbian."[34]

Redefining motherhood

The dilemma that women continue to face, of career or children or both, has to be eliminated if young women are to achieve their rightful ambitions. It is wrong that young women like Mary Gartrell should be faced with thinking themselves selfish because they are determined to pursue fulfilling careers at the expense of experiencing biological motherhood. Why should Mary Gartrell have to write that she is too *selfish* to give up years of her life and career for childbearing and rearing? It is hardly selfish of any person, male or female, young or old, to desire intense involvement in a vocation. Certainly Diana Forward is confident that she would be able to have career and children too, bringing them up alone. Yet for this to be a feasible proposition, our society must change drastically.

Firstly, the attitude that children are deprived unless they have an all-encompassing relationship with their mother has to be overcome. Such a relationship has drawbacks not only for the mother, but for the children also. It can be stultifying for both. As well, Dinnerstein and Chodorow have convincingly demonstrated in their studies that the concentrated mother-child relationship demanded of women and children in western society has long-lasting detrimental effects: it is at the base of our sexist society.[35] If patriarchal attitudes are to end, mothering must be redefined to include parenting by fathers on an equal level.

Secondly, the attitude that children are deprived unless they have both mother and father and live in a nuclear family must be replaced by an understanding that children can have closeness with just one natural parent, and gain fulfilment from the closeness of relationships with others who are not necessarily biologically related. As Emel Corley says, what is important is that more than one adult should take responsibility for the care of a child, and children should feel security, stability and love from the adults caring for them. Varieties of ways of living together are possible, and they should be encouraged. All women and men have a right to be involved in the upbringing of children, if they wish it and are prepared to make a responsible and caring commitment. This involvement should not be dependent upon biological parenthood. In acknowledging this, biological parents should also recognise that the love a child develops for another person is positive and does not detract from the love the child feels for them. This may well be one of the most difficult hurdles to overcome: parenting has been so closely allied to ownership of children that it will not be easy to renounce, despite that renunciation being in the better interests of children.

Flexibility and acceptance of non-traditional living arrangements must be the key. As Lee Mackay writes, "sharemothering" is one possibility:

> Sharemothering groups would not simply replace single parent or other nuclear families in feminist communities as they now exist. Our communities would be very different, because almost all of their members would be mothers, and thus vividly aware of the needs of children. When we held educational events, we would make sure that the children learned as much as the adults, and when we had celebrations, we would see that the children had as much fun as we did. We would develop many resources for our children — resources such as children's buildings, children's conferences, radical children's newspapers, children's clubs, children's therapy groups, and children's summer camps. Collectives would alter their structures to make it easy for mothers to work with them ... Since the communities in which we sharemothered would be so different from the communities in which some of us now mother, sharemothering would be far less onerous and isolating than mothering is at present.[36]

Another possibility is a redesigned "nuclear family", with parties being equal, and community support readily available when mother and/or father wish to take time off from mothering. But sharemothering and a redesigned nuclear family are not incompatible with one another. They can exist within the one society, and the same people may at different periods of their lives participate in both lifestyles. They do not have to oust other forms of shared parenting, single parenting and communal living. Nor do they preclude the single lifestyle or adults living together or in groups without children.

The optimum solution, however, can come about only with

changes in the workplace, taking place side by side with changes to family structures and parenting responsibilities and attitudes. Flexible hours would enable fathers, mothers, friends, aunts, co-dwellers, grandparents to organise their schedules to take into account their own needs, career needs, and children with whom they are involved. Maternity leave and parental leave should be written into the terms and conditions of all occupations. Women should no longer be penalised for taking time off during pregnancy and after giving birth.[35] The responsibility of men in the caring process should also be recognised and given credence in the workplace as well as at home.

Finally, the right of women not to bear children must be legally and socially acknowledged. This includes the right of women to live singly without children; in a close relationship with another person and without children; or collectively without bearing children. Women must be enabled to control their own bodies, and the right to decide when or whether to give birth is crucial to that control. Jennifer Stott says it is important to "question your motives" in the decision to bear a child. The questioning can only come about, and the motives be clearly seen, where women control their reproductivity. Readily available contraception and the right to choose an abortion, as well as the right of women not to be subjected to sexual intercourse without consent — in marriage or out of it — cannot be overlooked in the fight to create a world where all women are truly able to exercise choice in relation to their way of life, and where every child born is a wanted child.

Mary Gartrell

Mary Gartrell *was sixteen years old at the time of writing, and still at high school, looking toward a career in the science and maths fields.*

*P*ossibly the biggest influence from the beginning of my life has been my immediate family — both my brothers and my parents have played a large part in bringing me up feminist. My two older brothers have always been influential in my choice of clothes and actions. I couldn't keep up with them, climbing, running, if I was wearing a dress, and so I always wore jeans and shorts. Because I admired my brothers I always tried to copy them — their attitudes, their music. It was my brothers, along with my mother, who supported me when I was criticised for not shaving my legs. They agreed with me that it was unnecessary and a waste of time. My mother and father offered me dresses to wear when I was younger and we were going out. I refused to wear them because I could not move easily in them, and also my brothers teased me. So, my parents realised it was difficult for me and accepted it was more practical for me to wear jeans and shorts. Even now, at sixteen, I hate wearing dresses and feel uncomfortable in them.

I have never had to do much housework. My parents have

always accepted that spending a lot of time on music and reading is good use of my time. My brothers have always done more housework than I, but have never felt they were sissies because they were sweeping floors or cooking meals.

My parents have always shared housework, according to what needs to be done and what skills or physical problems they have. For example, my father does the washing because it is too hard on my mother's back. When one parent is busy with work or study, the other takes over the housework — cooking or general cleaning.

All three of us children have been brought up to help in everything when possible. What jobs we do doesn't matter so long as everything is done. It makes more sense for the boys to mow lawns and do heavy labouring jobs, because they are older and stronger than I, whereas I can manage the washing up and sweeping floors. Now both brothers live away from home and are very good cooks. I think they are glad to have had the chance to learn to manage their households. In this, I have always been aware that my family and home are quite different from the households of many of my friends and schoolmates. My immediate family has not been the only influence on my attitudes towards women and their place in the community. I have many cousins, most of whom are female. I always have, and still do, admire them very much. Our families have been close and shared many holidays, so I have had continual contact with people of my own age and values, sharing a feminist viewpoint.

Being a feminist for me means more job opportunities, more independence, as well as more free time and leisure activities. My mother and aunts have all run their own businesses very successfully. One aunt is in an important public office. All are capable of running their lives and businesses. They have proved to me that women can run an organisation and cope with difficult situations just as well as some men can. It depends on personality and ability, not on what sex you are.

It has been important for me to see "normal" women doing a wide range of jobs. I have no particular hero whom I see myself following although some people's achievements have inspired me to follow their lead. When I was about eight years old I was very impressed by a neighbour, three years older than I, who played the trumpet. She played the solo part and was appearing in the Opera House; I realised I would like to be like her. So I took up the trumpet and was encouraged by my parents and my primary school teachers. Playing the trumpet requires a lot of energy and physical strength, as well as strong lungs. I needed that encouragement and was thrilled when it was my turn to be like the girl who played in the Opera House.

The women around me, doing things, have probably had the largest subconscious effect on me. They have shown you don't have to be a superwoman or a "radical" to have a career other than being a housewife or nurse. I can see they enjoy their work and are capable of doing the job.

I had never thought about getting married until I was about ten years old. I then decided definitely against it. All I could see were all the disadvantages of marriage. (At that stage marriage was connected in my mind to having children. My brothers were fifteen and sixteen and fought and argued with each other, and with my parents.) I decided there were just too many difficulties, and thought marriage and those who got married were "dumb". Now I might consider marriage if I met the right sort of person, but I would probably find a de facto relationship more appropriate. I don't want to have children and see marriage (still) going hand in hand with having them. Not wanting children, I don't see the point of getting married. Society now accepts people living in de facto relationships, and I think more and more people should consider that arrangement before marriage. Marrying is a big decision, and at the age of twenty or so I don't think I could commit myself to one person for the rest of my life without knowing them very well.

I do not see marriage as the antithesis of feminism. If the man agrees with the notion of equal opportunities for women and is supportive, the relationship can work well. My parents are such an example. Both partners must be tolerant of each other's feelings and differences of opinion. Marriage should not rule out individual points of view. There may be problems, but I think they can be overcome through tolerance and discussion.

Although I love children and have had lots of experience looking after them, at all ages, I would rather they weren't mine. I cannot see myself being able to bring up children as well and as carefully as my mother and father, yet have an interesting and exciting career. What I know of childcare services, even the good ones, I don't think they can take the place of parents or be as good as they are.

My mother had to stay at home for some years looking after her children, and I am too selfish to give up years of my life and career for that. The father is just as important as the mother in caring for a child. My father has always been very affectionate towards my brothers and me. We still kiss our parents goodnight, or goodbye, and I think this affection from both is important to our relationship. I appreciate what my parents did for my brothers and me, and while I am grateful to them, I know I could not do the same.

That a lot of women have had to, and still do, choose either to have a career or a family is terribly sexist and unfair. Because the mother bears the child should not mean she has also to be the one who forgoes a career to rear the child. I realise males usually get paid at a better rate than females, so the mother staying home makes economic sense. I think it needs a superwoman and a superman to have careers and children simultaneously.

The main influences on my choice of career are, and have ever been, my interests and what I am skilled at. My school, a girls' school, has always encouraged girls to consider trades as well as academic pursuits. Our careers adviser is a relatively young woman. She is keen that we select the area we are most interested in, so she presents every possible avenue. When we make a choice, we are encouraged and given all material and information we need. The adviser is well informed and up to date on the job market; she is aware of opportunities for women at the moment, and also of the pressures of sexism existing in some areas.

For two years we discuss careers on a weekly basis and go on excursions to all open days at the universities. Being at a selective school means more people want to do some sort of tertiary education than is usual in lots of secondary schools. This means there are few from my school who follow trades.

I have had many ideas about what I want to do "when I grow up". As a small child I wanted to do the things I saw on television and the jobs I had heard and knew about — for instance, a teacher, a nurse or a hostess. But as I got more information and my schooling continued, I became more interested in following my aptitude for maths and science, seeming to follow in my father's and brother's footsteps. My father has always been ready to talk about science and his work, and so has my brother about his university course. The discussions at home, at the end of the day, about how the day has gone, have greatly influenced me. This also influenced my choice of subjects in senior high school.

The support I have received from other women has enabled me to maintain and enjoy my feminist views. Some of my friends feel the same way about clothes and shaving of legs as I do, so on outings I am not alone with my tastes. Some friends are not feminists, and a couple claim to be anti-feminist, so we have many discussions about the importance of appearance, articles of clothing such as high-heeled shoes, and how such pressures are not placed on men. I have lots of support for my viewpoints from my mother, her friends (many of whom are in the Women's Electoral Lobby and other groups), as well as from relatives and a few friends. I think that at my age, being a feminist is still considered to be a bit radical. Certainly in my group of friends I find myself defending my point of view quite often. On reflection I believe the number of feminists in my age group is growing because more and more women can see that by broadening their outlook, by accepting feminist values, they can lead a more enjoyable life and have more variety in how they live and work.

Diana Forward

Diana Forward, *a student at the University of Melbourne, was living in Italy when her piece was written, doing "typical female jobs" like waitressing and chambermaiding.*

It is almost stating the obvious to say that one's beliefs are influenced by family background. My family background, much as I may hate to admit it at times, certainly played a great part in forming the opinions I hold today. Home life was never quite the suburban norm. My earliest memories are of three or four years of age. Then, my mother was a teacher at the local high school in Canberra. When I was about six we moved to Melbourne and Mum, instead of continuing to work, went back to university. I was lucky because I was never really exposed to the idea that a woman's place was in the home. It seemed natural to me that women should lead autonomous lives with interests outside the home, whether or not they were married, with kids. I also believed academic achievement was within a woman's reach. I assumed everybody, male or female, went to university when they "grew up". My parents certainly weren't the type to think education was not important for a girl.

Housework was another area which was perhaps different

from the norm. It was shared between my mother and father (if it was done at all!) and the jobs we children had to do were never allocated on the basis of "you're a girl, he's a boy". If I had to make my bed, my brother had to make his. My father cooked our breakfasts and made our lunches while we were at primary school so I never assumed the kitchen was solely a woman's responsibility.

I was always sensitive about anything that could possibly be construed as sexist and the slightest hint of it was enough to put me on my soapbox for hours. However, I am unsure where the sensitivity came from. Certainly both my parents were against sexual inequality but I don't recall any discussions on anything along those lines being held until after I had "become a feminist". I remember I hated my sister and I collectively being called "the girls". It seemed we were being degraded because of our sex. It was taking away our individuality and our right to have our views respected. In reality it meant nothing of the sort, or so I was assured. However, whether that was the intention or not was beside the point to me. After all, much sexism is carried out unintentionally because it's a way of life. Unintentional sexism is probably the most dangerous of all.

I remember one time when we were all sitting around at home and my father asked my mother, "What's for tea?" That enraged me. He had no right to assume she should prepare the meal, that it was her responsibility. He was quite astounded at my fury. He hadn't meant anything, but that is precisely my point. If one assumes it is a woman's duty to prepare the meals, and accepts the assumption blindly, the situation will continue. It is only by beginning to question, that reason can be introduced and equality established.

Another aspect of my family life contributing to making me what I am now is that I was not brought up on "girls' toys" — dolls and teasets. Toys are sickening in the way they condition children, preparing them for their future roles. My mother was very much against this and caused a scandal at a Duntroon Christmas party one year. Since my father worked there, we went to the Christmas parties held every year. Father Christmas came in his helicopter, giving out presents to all the children. Presents were selected according to the age and sex of the child and when my brother, then about seven years old, was given a toy gun and I, about four years old, a teaset, Mum was livid with rage and tore strips off all responsible. At the time, all I was worried about was not having my present but I'm sure her attitudes had their effect. I didn't grow up dreaming of the day I'd marry and have a kitchen "just like Mummy".

Family background contributed in many other ways. I knew many women who lived away from the traditional mould. My world as a child was certainly not sexist. It would have been quite difficult for me *not* to grow up a feminist.

Marriage is one thing I was always against, although probably more for itself than because of any feminist objections. I swore black and blue I would never marry and my opinion hasn't changed much since. However, that doesn't mean I believe marriage is incompatible with a feminist lifestyle. It's not marriage itself that oppresses women, at least not today. Instead it is the way the marriage is treated that counts. Although to me there is not much point in getting married, the wife of today does not have to take on the role of slave to her house, husband and children unless she is stupid enough to choose to do so. Marriage is really a dead issue to me now. A woman is no longer placed in the despicable situation of being obliged by society, practically and morally, to marry before she leaves home, before she has children, before she does anything, and she no longer has to rely on a husband or father to support her. There is no longer any *need* to get married, as opposed to the desire to do so, and there is no longer any need for marriage to mean oppression of women. You either get married or you don't, and that's the end of it.

Children are a slightly different matter because children are, by force of nature, dependent on their "caretaker", at least up until a certain age. However, this doesn't mean that women have to choose between children or a career. There are numerous options. A woman can have children on her own either looking after them herself full-time, or relying on creches, childcare centres, family or friends to take care of the child while she works. If the situation allows it, she could take the child to work with her. She can have children with a partner. Then the choice is between which of the two does what. The possibilities are practically endless.

I want to have children and want to bring them up myself. That does not mean I intend to sacrifice having a career. I will just have to plan carefully. My problem is that Robert, the person with whom I will probably be having these as yet hypothetical children, also wants to be involved full-time in "parenting" while I go out to work. Obviously, some sort of compromise will have to be worked out.

In general, the main problem arises if a woman has a particularly demanding career requiring "twenty-four hours a day" dedication and the probability of not being home often. It would be handy to have a partner prepared to stay at home full-time with the children, a reversal of the traditional roles. Other than that, the only solution I see is to start your career after your children have become a little independent because, after all, if you decide to have children you have a responsibility towards them and once you've made the choice you have no right to be flippant with their lives.

As for career, I have not made up my mind. I always wanted to be a teacher. At primary school it was a primary school teacher; at high school, a high school teacher; and after moving to Coburg, a remedial English teacher. The trouble is that everybody else seems to think teaching is a waste of time and they have all tried to persuade me to do something else. At times, I admit, it worries me that teaching is such a "woman's job" and I think I ought to choose another career — one not traditionally a woman's domain.

Right now the other career interesting me is law, with the benefit of being a predominantly male profession. I was talked into considering law by my Higher School Certificate legal studies teacher, who is concerned about the lack of women in the legal profession. However, if I decide to study law next year, it will be with the aim of becoming a barrister. I don't think I could settle for becoming a solicitor. It's in no way because I'm ambitious, but because I feel that to become a barrister would perhaps be a small "victory" for women, whereas becoming a solicitor is no victory at all. It is still relegating women to second place — like becoming a nurse instead of a doctor, a secretary instead of a manager, or a dental assistant instead of a dentist, as far too many women do.

I get the same feeling when people look at me, see I'm female, and ask what my occupation is. I can tell they're assuming hairdresser, clerk, or something along those lines, and when I reply I'm a uni student they are stunned for a fraction of a second (a girl with brains?). Recovering themselves, they reply, "Oh really, Latrobe?"

On the whole, though, I think things are improving for

women. Girls are encouraged more to take up maths-science courses at school, at one time almost a taboo, and are able to choose from the entire spectrum of careers. What hurts me most is when a girl says she wants to be a hairdresser or a nurse, not from any great desire or lack of ability to do anything else, but simply from the conditioning she has received — an over-dose of *Dolly* magazines. Maybe that's a rather bourgeois attitude, but I feel it's such a waste, an act of self-degradation.

"Other women" as groups is one thing I have had almost nothing to do with. I am supportive of other women in my beliefs and my contact with them as individuals. However, I feel slightly hostile towards many of the organised feminist groups. I object to the way they try to make women's liberation an issue for women only. The feminist club at Melbourne University is one example. They hold meetings every Thursday (or whenever they are) in "the women's room" — all women welcome. Those very women who propose to believe in equality of the sexes are actually saying that there is a legitimate difference between the sexes. In a way, they are excluding men from the fight, saying that men can't and/or don't want to be feminists. This is not true. It is unfair, even self-defeating. I believe feminism is an issue that ought to concern every one of us.

So, I am more involved with other women as individuals. If I can persuade somebody that certain aspects of her migrant upbringing are wrong — for example, that she does not have to obey her husband, she is not his inferior and that she doesn't even have to have a husband at all — if I can help her respect herself and break away from the sexist aspects of her condition-ing, then hopefully I have achieved more than a year's mem-bership of a feminist group.

I couldn't say there have been any specific people who have had a profound effect on me, as far as women's rights are concerned, nor have there been any particular events I could isolate as particularly meaningful, except perhaps a BBC television series called *Shoulder to Shoulder* which I saw in England when I was about nine. It was a history of the Pank-hurst family, and the suffragette movement. Strangely, I don't think I can remember any of the facts but I can still feel my horror, frustration and anger as I watched the treatment of those women, and the pride and admiration their actions inspired in me. I think it was at that moment I felt the urge to continue their struggle and now, as I write, remembering them makes me feel guilty that I have done so little.

Perhaps I was concerned about the situation of women earlier than anything else, but I am also concerned about other major issues, unfortunately stereotyped for a "young radical feminist" — Aborigines, the class struggle, conservation, nuclear disarmament. The main problem I face, however, is working out how to actually *achieve* anything in even one of these areas. The difficulties are so infinitely large and the solutions seemingly nonexistent. I can vote, but will my choice or representation be allowed to govern, or be allowed to make any meaningful changes? I can march in demonstrations, sign petitions, join hundreds of clubs, political parties, movements; I can supposedly do numerous things, but what can I achieve? Can I prevent a nuclear war or stop industrial waste choking the world I live in? At the moment I see no positive answers and therefore no hope for the future. Small changes may be brought about in this area and that, but will anything ever be really different? I don't really know what I can do — and all my other concerns fall into second place behind that.

Looking away from the world and its problems as a whole, slowly, slowly the situation seems to be improving for women. However, there is still a discouragingly long way to go. In places like Australia I can look around and feel slightly optimistic. But then I come to Italy and in the little village where I am staying now, the majority of women have no conception of rights to equality between the sexes. To achieve anything here you have to break through hundreds of years of the same way of life, through religion and superstition that refuse to accept a new way of thinking. The advances of each new generation are stifled by the presence of the last.

Here, it is not uncommon to hand out bloodstained sheets the day after a wedding to show the town that the new wife was a virgin, and the situation is many times worse in other parts of Italy, and other parts of the world. However, even here there is hope if we keep up the fight, although it may take another fifty, one hundred years. The question is, will the world survive long enough for us to succeed?

CHAPTER FIVE

Influences

... as respects their daughters, [parents] have nothing to do with the unjustice of laws, nor the absurdities of society. Their duty is plain, evident, decided. In a daughter they have in charge a human being; in a son, the same. Let them train up these human beings, under the expaned wings of liberty. Let them seek for them and with them just knowledge; encouraging, from the cradle upwards, that useful curiosity which will lead them unbidden in the paths of free enquiry; and place them, safe and superior to the storms of life, in the security of ... self-possessed minds, well grounded, well reasoned, conscientious opinions, and self-approved, consistent practice.

Frances Wright,
Course of Popular Lectures, 1829

Call on God, my dear, She will help you.

Mrs O. H. P. Belmont,
to a discouraged young suffragist,
circa 1917-1918, in Doris Stevens,
Jailed for Freedom, 1920

I'd gone through life believing in the strength and competence of others; never in my own. Now, dazzled, I discovered that my capacities were real. It was like finding a fortune in the lining of an old coat.

Joan Mills,
"What Women Say About Themselves"
in Women, Women, Women — Quips,
Quotes, and Commentary,
Leta W. Clark, editor, 1977

Not all young women grow up expressing adherence to feminist ideals. As Mary Gartrell, living on Sydney's North Shore, writes, some of her friends are supportive of her, though not all of them are feminists; some even claim to be anti-feminist. Many girls no doubt grow up knowing little of the

truth of feminism: Karen Ermacora points out that some
adults misunderstand it; and Cathy Henry and Sarah Gillman
agree that many people's vision of feminism is restricted to
stereotypical views about appearance: feminists are exclusively
boilersuited with close cropped hair and hobnailed boots. The
media has never forgotten the (wrongly) reported burning of a
bra at the Anti-Miss America rally, and the phrase has
haunted "women's libbers" ever since.

With the lack of understanding of and knowledge about
feminism and feminist history, it is surprising that some young
women do perceive the message. Despite the conscious and
unconscious efforts that are made by the culture of patriarchy
to hide women's history, the message gets through. But many
young women do not realise the tremendous efforts that have
been made by women (and by some men) through the ages to
ensure that women's achievements are not lost absolutely but
remain in documents, however dusty, and in minds, however
old, ready to be dusted off, delved into, questioned. As Mary
Stott, one of the feisty, outspoken, assertive, aggressive,
indomitable, glorious old women interviewed by Dale Spender
in her book on the longevity of the women's movement has
said, "There's always been a women's movement this century!"[1]
And in *Women of Ideas — and What Men Have Done to
Them*, Dale Spender has, through her diligent scholarship,
illustrated that "a women's movement" has existed in the
Anglo-tradition for at least three hundred years. She writes:

> For years I had not thought to challenge the received wisdom
> of my own history tutors who had — in the only fragment of
> knowledge about angry women I was ever endowed with —
> informed me that early in the twentieth century, a few un-
> balanced and foolish women had chained themselves to rail-
> ings in the attempt to obtain the vote. When I learnt, how-
> ever, that in 1911 there had been twenty-one regular
> feminist periodicals in Britain . . ., that there was a feminist
> book shop, a women's press, and a women's bank run by and
> for women, I could no longer accept that the reason I knew
> almost nothing about women of the past was because there
> were so few of them, and they had done so little. I began to
> acknowledge not only that the women's movement of the
> early twentieth century was bigger, stronger and more influ-
> ential than I had ever suspected, but that it might not have

been the *only* such movement. It was in this context that I
began to wonder whether the disappearance of the women
of the past was an accident . . .[2]

Who are the women who have disappeared or have been kept
from us, and from our daughters? The beginnings of the
answer lie in determining who are the "prominent women", the
women who have been "left in". Queen Elizabeth I is difficult
to hide, particularly as she ruled Britain during its most
prominent mercantile period — the Americas were "discovered", trading grew and multiplied, the English became supreme
on the seas. Florence Nightingale is allowed to be shown in
schoolbooks as a woman of some resource and courage. In our
own history, Caroline Chisholm is much talked about — and
even allowed to be remembered by all who care to look at the
reverse side of the five dollar note. So, say the (male)
luminaries, what's the problem? You have your women. There
may be far fewer of them than prominent men, but that
accords with reality.

   The problem is threefold. Firstly, the number of prominent
women of whom we are permitted to know is not a true figure
of the women who have been active, important, first-rate
thinkers, innovators, inventors and geniuses throughout the
centuries. Although there no doubt have been fewer such
women than men, because men controlled the resources which
could allow individuals of that ilk to develop, many more
women broke through the ranks than have come down to us
through the pages of history. Secondly, those women of whom
we learn are depicted as exceptions: there are few of them,
goes the tale, because most women are pedestrian or mediocre;
most women are incapable of making it. Not only are they
exceptions. They are eccentrics, too. Peculiar. Odd. Old
maids. Virgin queens. Young girls sometimes are forced to
endure the story that Queen Elizabeth was "not really a
woman, you know" in whisperings around the classroom.
Florence Nightingale was "really a lesbian" (as if the state is
negative, and negates her every deed). Anyway, Florence
Nightingale established nursing as a women's occupation (and
would never have been able to do so without the advice,
support and energies of Sir Sydney Herbert, a man of course)
and advised clearly that nurses should at all times play the
subservient role, maidservant to the (male) doctor. Finally, the

very concept of prominent women (or men) is suspect: who determines prominence? what characteristics denote "importance"? why should prominent men (or women) be worthy of reporting, and all others be ignored? Masculine standards determine the characteristics for which individuals should be remembered, and ignore the work of the many who work in the background; they concentrate upon the economic elite, those of high birth and the intellectual elite (where "intellectual" has its own narrow meaning, and cleverly excludes those who have no access to resources to develop it).

The mediocrity of women has been emphasised throughout history, in the rare times that attention has been paid to female members of society. It is not only in the schoolrooms of today that women teachers and girl students have been classed in this way. In 1928 Dorothy Brock wrote of girls' schools in England:

"The special danger of girls' schools," says the ... *Report [of the Consultative Committee on the Differentiation of the Curriculum,* published in 1923] "is that they may become excellently organised and conscientiously loyal groups, composed of mediocre and uniform units." I have a feeling that that sentence was written by a man; it does not fairly describe the schools which I know and in which I have lived. I do not really believe girls are always more imitative and "uniform" than boys; the tyranny of tradition in a boys' preparatory school, for instance, is one of the most cast-iron tyrannies in the world. And I sometimes wonder whether the impression that girls are so monotonously "conscientious" is not an out-worn cliche ...[3]

Even where women are criminal and therefore classified as acting contrary not only to the law, but also to "natural laws" (that is, the supposition that women will not act antisocially as often as will men), their mediocrity as criminals is often remarked upon. Indeed, it has founded some theories of women's criminality. Thus Caesare Lombroso, one of the first criminologists to write about the female offender, drew up categories of women as criminals.[4] A very small number of them, in his view, fitted into the "born criminal" category. Here, they were physically unattractive, with dark hair, body hair, large craniums, prominent jaws, and strode about in a swashbuckling way (a decidedly negative trait for a woman!);

they offended against the criminal law and against the feminine role of women. The larger category of female offender was that of the "occasional criminal". She was physically like most other women — that is, "feminine" — and her problem arose from her compliant nature, her psychological weakness, lack of understanding about standards of private property ownership, and desire for fripperies and furbelows making her susceptible to indulging in minor crimes such as shoplifting. The reason so few women were criminal compared with men was, in Lombroso's theory, due to female passivity, lack of originality, and plain mediocrity.

Where women are not so easily classed as mediocre, but rise to prominence, it is not long before the majority of them are firmly relegated to the ranks of those who simply cannot be spoken of or written about. Dale Spender illustrates well this process in relation to numerous women. She writes:

> Women *are* intellectually competent, and even the repudiating devices of patriarchy cannot always conceal this. But even where women's intellectual competence is "undeniable", men are still able to "deny" it, and take it away. Women who reveal their intellectual resources are often described as having "masculine minds", which is a clever device for acknowledging their contribution while at the same time it allows it to be dismissed, for a woman with a "masculine mind" is unrepresentative of her sex, and the realm of the intellectual is still retained by men.
>
> Even when we display our power to think in terms men havè validated, to follow their arguments and reach their conclusions, we will rarely receive "credit" for it. Once again our existence can be dismissed even at the point at which we display it. For the consensus will invariably be that it was not *reason* that we used to arrive at our conclusions, but a much inferior, capricious and lucky process — *intuition*. Again, men retain their ownership of the mental world by this classification, and women's intellectual competence is denied.[5]

Spender's examples include Aphra Behn, who wrote seventeen plays, produced over a seventeen-year period in London, beginning with her first play, *The Forced Marriage* or *The Jealous Bridegroom* in September 1670. She wrote thirteen novels, "thirty years before Daniel Defoe wrote *Robinson*

Crusoe, generally termed the first novel". She published collections of poems and translated other works. Aphra Behn was a political activist, feminist, and agitator for the abolition of slavery. She was derided for her views by the literary establishment (despite the considerable popularity of her plays and writings), and frequently accused of plagiarism. She was criticised for not taking the expected female role of remaining silent, a good and comely partner to a man; *he* should star, not she (she never married). The fact that she was a woman was used to discredit her, her detractors using a familiar technique, that of casting doubt upon her chastity. In 1862 a reviewer wrote, under the title "Literary Garbage" in the *Saturday Review* of 27 January:

> Mrs Behn is still to be found here and there in the dusty worm eaten libraries of old country houses, but as a rule we imagine she has been ejected from all *decent* society for more than a generation or two. If Mrs Behn is read at all, it can only be from a love of impurity for its own sake, for rank indecency . . . even in her own day. Mrs Behn's works had a scandalous reputation . . . it is true that this did not prevent her from attaining honourable burial in Westminster Abbey but it is a pity her books did not rot with her bones. That they should now be disinterred from obscurity into which they have happily fallen is surely inexcusable.

Mary Wollstonecraft's work was similarly rejected: in 1799 the *Historical Magazine* said her work should be read "with disgust by any female who has any pretensions to delicacy; with detestation by everyone attached to the interests of religion and morality, and with indignation by anyone who might feel any regard for the unhappy woman, whose frailties should have been buried in oblivion".

History also conceals the activism of women in numerous causes, not the least in the feminist cause. Thus, when women complain today of sexist language and the imposition of male forms of language upon women by way of the argument that "man" is a generic term, and that in law "he" includes "she", they are told their objections are foolish and empty; the implication (and often the explicit statement) is that language has always been written and spoken thus. This is untrue. Before the mid-nineteenth century it was not accepted in law

that the masculine included the feminine form. From the
sixteenth century in England grammarians pursued a path of
promoting the masculine form above the feminine (they did
not believe "man" included "woman"; to them, woman was far
inferior and to bestow the term "man" upon any woman was to
elevate her far above her station). The rationale was that the
masculine form was superior to the feminine. In 1553 T.
Wilson asserted in *Arte of Rhetorique*:

> Some will set the Carte before the horse, as thus. My mother
> and my father are both at home, even as thoughe the good
> man of the house ware no breaches, or that the graye Mare
> were the better Horse. And what thoughe it often so happen-
> neth (God wotte the more pite) yet in speaking at leaste, let
> us kepe a natural order, and set the man before the woman
> for maners Sake.[6]

According to Wilson, linguistic ordering of female and male
should give the male priority, for "the worthier is preferred and
set before. As a man is sette before a woman".

Some writers followed this principle in the seventeenth
century, in accordance with the same sentiments. The first
advocacy of the "rule" that the masculine was the more worthy
— and that, further, it should subsume the feminine, so that
women need not be spoken of but incorporated within the masculine form, came in 1746. Rule 21 of J. Kirby's syntactic rules,
set out in *A New English Grammar*, provided:

> The masculine Person answers to the general Name, which
> comprehends both Male and Female; as Any Person who
> knows what he says.[7]

Yet this was by no means generally accepted in the eighteenth
century. W. Ward in *An Essay on Grammar* explicitly ruled
out any need for adopting the "masculine includes the
feminine" approach, saying:

> ... *he* must represent a male; *she* a female; and it, an
> object of no sex ... But the plural *they* equally represents
> objects of all the three genders; for a plural object may
> consist of singular objects, some of which are masculine,
> others feminine and others neuter; as, a man and a woman
> and some iron were in the waggon, and they were all over-
> turned ...

This frees English, in a great measure, from the per-
plexity of such rules, as "the masculine gender is more
worthy than the feminine ..." neither the English adjec-
tives, nor the plural personal, nor the plural possessive
pronouns have a distinction of gender.[8]

Other scholars, including Catherine Macaulay and Elizabeth
Murray, protested in more broad-ranging terms. Finally, the
battle was lost when the *Acts Interpretation Act* of 1850 was
passed in the United Kingdom (and applying in the Australian
colonies) to provide:

... In all Acts words importing the masculine gender shall
be deemed and taken to include females, and the singular to
include the plural, and the plural the singular, unless the
contrary as to gender and number is expressly provided.

This legal ruling did not have full community support. Women
(and some men) questioned the rule. Indeed, even some courts
declined at times to follow it, including "she" within "he" if
criminal acts were outlawed, but excluding "she" if benefits
were to be gained by a law. Courts also evaded the rule, when
they chose, by holding that "person" did not include women, if
"persons" were granted some benefit or privilege by a
particular law. Protests against the legal ruling and against
court decisions manipulating it continued throughout the
century and into the twentieth century.

Similarly, the battle for the vote in Australia has been
depicted in establishment histories as involving no work on the
part of women. Rather, the picture painted is that women sat
passively by, whilst parliamentarians graciously bestowed upon
them the right to vote in federal and state elections. This is far
removed from the truth. Women in all states fought for the
right to vote. One of the many was Brettena Smyth, who
became active in the movement in the early 1890s in Victoria.
She wrote and lectured on issues such as women's role —
particularly in marriage, birth control, women's political rights
and legal standing, and women's lack of economic equality.
Farley Kelly reports:

... she was to be found "conspicuous in blue-shaded
goggles" delivering a "sharply constructed address" on the
need for women's suffrage on the classic ground of No Tax-

ation without Representation. She had performed the major
duties of the citizen for seventeen years, paying rates and
taxes, running both business and family single-handed; and
she could not see why she should be denied a voice in the
government of the state . . .[9]

Again, the method used to deny credibility to these women was
that of decrying them on sexual grounds. One parliamentarian
was observed as remarking that there was nothing so admirable
as "a beautiful noble woman discharging her duty in the sick-
room, [but] there is another class, the raw-boned long-bearded
ones that I do not want to come into contact with at the ballot
box or anywhere else".

Today, the view is promoted that only a small cluster of
today's women protest strictures placed on women in relation
to dress and adornment. Yet in the nineteenth century women
in the United States and England rebelled against the vol-
uminous skirts they were supposed by convention to wear,
donning bloomers. (If this is brought to attention today, it is
mainly for the purpose of ridiculing the women for what were
sensible efforts to ensure that women could move freely about,
unhampered by metres of material.) And in Australia, the
"rational dress" movement of the same period had its feminist
adherents. As well, Louisa Lawson (rarely mentioned by historians or in literary anthologies, unless as the mother of
Henry) wrote on the "beauty cult" and the dangers of wearing
high heels. On 1 July 1891 in her newspaper, *The Dawn*, she
wrote:

A great many women who buy or fashion their own
headgear, seem to proceed upon the idea that in point of
value, the bonnet is more than the head, and the hat more
than the face; or that the head is a mere knob, upon which
to display millinery. This must account for the masses of
lace, feathers, frippery, and even parts of deceased fowls,
that partly cover, or are skewered to the many female heads.
The object of anything more is presumed to be for
protection or for ornament, and to combine the two is
supposed to belong to the art of the milliner.
    Worth, the Parisien Mantua-maker, once remarked to a
woman, as he was arranging a bunch of flowers on the skirt
of a gown, "You must not think that all these befrilled and
trumpery things are of my taste. They are not my taste at all.

I make them because you will have them" . . .

[Bonnets] such as from size, shape and trimming are so pronounced, monstrous and extraordinary as to leave the head under them comparatively of no account whatever in the way of interest, should be avoided by the would-be purchaser who cannot afford a new outlay every month in the year.[10]

Women's history is also distorted by the omission of other truths. Debates about the alleged inability of women to perform in particular professions exclude the fact that women were precluded by law for many years from doing so. This is also true in the parliamentary sphere, where women fought for the right to enter parliaments around Australia. In the 1890s Catherine Spence was the first Australian woman to stand for Parliament when she sought election to the South Australian Assembly. One of her major planks was "effective voting", based on quota representation.[11]

The role model debate

This lack of education about women's history is important because it deprives all women of a base from which to progress: not knowing what has gone before, they are unaware of the ways in which their own efforts to improve the status of women may be negated in the future; they lose sight of (or never gain) the very real possibility that their work is *presently* losing its impact because masculine methods of derogation are being used minute by minute, hour by hour and day by day to excise their very real achievements. The process described by Dale Spender as being used in the past to denigrate women who were prominent, learned, profound thinkers or writers is no less effective today. Thus we are confronted with media stories of the "renunciation" by Betty Friedan and Germaine Greer of their previously firmly stated views of women's rights and feminism. Greer and Friedan are depicted as feminist turncoats — and unfortunately many women accept this.

Yet, when *Sex and Destiny* and *The Second Stage* are read, despite the attempts of the dominant culture to negate them, it becomes clear that Greer and Friedan cannot and should not be so easily dismissed. How many of Greer's original readers agreed with every word she wrote in *The Female Eunuch*? How many disagreed with nothing which appeared between the covers of Friedan's first feminist tract, *The Feminine Mystique*? Is there any obligation upon any one of us to agree with every word of their later writings? That we find disagreement should not lead to an automatic dismissal of the entire contents of the later work, nor a revision of thought about the earlier work, dismissing it now that both authors have somehow become "unsafe" for feminists to admire. Rather than be so easily enmeshed in an about-turn manufactured by those who wish, consciously or unconsciously, to dismiss powerful women theorists and writers as "untouchable", girls and women must learn to resist the trap laid out for them, and recognise the need to be discerning. That we disagree today with those whom yesterday we saw as heroines does not dictate an inevitable dismissal of them to the "never-to-be-recalled" levels of consciousness. Why participate in efforts to deprive us of admired and admirable women?

Girls and women are too readily deprived of role models: there are few women who have evidently achieved great things; those who have, have been hidden as soon as it is decently possible for our culture to regroup its heros, leaving out the women. There are few women upon whom girls and women can model themselves, or who may act as their mentors. (Men and boys do not lack models, nor mentors.) Our society suffers from the syndrome of the "first woman": the "first woman engineer", the "first policewoman", the "first woman novelist — economist — lawyer — judge — teacher — trade union official . . .". For centuries, women have been having firsts, so as never, apparently, to go beyond the first, to the second, third, fourth, hundredth ... At regular intervals the world is confronted with an announcement of yet another first for women, creating the idea that any woman who does anything beyond the expected — marrying, having children, growing old, grandmothering, dying — is unusual, exceptional, and that her feat is a never-to-be-repeated event. Unfortunately, because women's history lacks the continuity so evident in the historical records of male performance and achievement, each new generation of women believes that the woman depicted as first is indeed a first, and that her achievement has no precedent. This lack of continuity leaves girls and women with no base upon which to build, creating a false picture of women in general as non-achievers, without the capacity to perform in any way other than those which are traditionally accepted as womanly.

Some role models do, however, make their way into the vision of young women who grow up feminist. Fortunately, the few role models who exist (or who are allowed to be perceived to exist) provide an impetus for girls growing up in a world where male achievements are more important than those of women and are less difficult to gain. (At least the world believes men *should* achieve in a multiplicity of ways.) Jennifer Stott, working in journalism, early discovered women writers and film-makers whom she admired and whose work had an important influence upon her development, among them Australians Judith Allen and Meaghan Morris, the British feminist Beatrix Campbell and New Yorker Fran Lebowitz. Diana Forward was prompted to learn more about the feminist struggle for the vote in England when she saw a television production of a history of that time, *Shoulder to Shoulder*, which depicted "ordinary" women fighting for enfranchise- ment alongside the Pankhursts and others more widely known than the thousands making up the troops. Anna Donald found Emily Pankhurst a hero, an inspiration for her progres- sion as a feminist. And with Sarah Gillman she shared an appreciation of Miles Franklin. Others wrote of Germaine Greer and Betty Friedan, and anthropologist Margaret Mead.

Sarah Gillman and Anna Donald discovered women's writ- ing and women's history when they wrote school assignments. Others were impressed by women politicians. Elizabeth Reid, appointed by the Whitlam Labor government in 1973 as women's advisor (reportedly the first appointment of its type to be made in Australia),[12] and Irene Greenwood, long-time Western Australian feminist, were crucial to Fiona Giles' appreciation of feminist ideology.

Yet what becomes overwhelmingly clear in the reading of each young woman's contribution is the prominent part played by peers and family members in their conceptions of feminism and their embrace of its design for living. This gives impetus to a possible reassessment of the "role model" disposition of current Australian feminism. Should so much of women's energies and hopes be directed toward creating role models for young women? Or is there a danger that in doing so, although it may spark off some striving to achieve to emulate the model, it promotes yet again the idea that some women are special and can make it; that some women are to be admired and looked up to — but, lacking their abilities or exceptional talents, those looking up admiringly cannot really aspire to those same heights? Too great a concentration upon the role model view of the world must leave many young women (and their older sisters) subdued — how can they possibly achieve *that*? The role model *must* be different to have gone so far in a hostile world.

If role models in what is seen as a masculine world of achievement are to play a useful part in promoting young women's desire to go beyond what has previously been dictated as woman's place, they must not allow themselves to be painted, falsely, as exceptional. What is important is that the achievers who *are* allowed through, into the male bastions, remain "of us". They must work hard to remain real, rather than isolating themselves where they, in turn, may be dealt with as Dale Spender describes in *Women of Ideas* — pilloried as "odd", and finally forgotten.[13]

Women at the top have not only to strive in their own terms for their own achievements, but have a responsibility to look back, with support — and not only to look! Some women — Irene Greenwood, Elizabeth Reid — manage this with grace and spirit. Fiona Giles has the impression of their wit and wisdom shining through in everyday situations, not spilling out from on high to those sitting, Platonic-student-like at their feet. The factor not to be forgotten is that women have been deprived of confidence and self-esteem. One way of recovering them is to know women who are confident, who exude self-esteem. But at the same time, this can be as daunting as the aura surrounding successful men, perhaps more so. And the picture created may well be false.

Thus, for young women growing up feminist, family and peer support, and family and peers as role models are imperative. The role models should, ideally, be male as well as female. Each of the contributors' stories shows the value of these models. Sarah Gillman is the eldest of three daughters, with a "strong, capable woman" as her mother. Mary Gartrell's parents and brothers supported her when she refused to bow to convention and shave her legs. Her parents shared housework and mother and aunts ran their own successful businesses. Michele Trewick's mother, though not defining herself a feminist, conveyed to her daughter the belief that women are equal with men, and that Michele was capable of doing what she wanted. All speak of a close female role model — a woman in the household — as essential to their feminist development.

Jennifer Stott writes of the support she gained in her profession as a journalist from her fellow workers. They appreciated her ideas and acted as mentors. Sarah Gillman found her headmistress an important role model. Peers are important to Mary Gartrell, who was impressed by a girl neighbour who was a musician, and took up playing the trumpet as a result. Emel Corley, writing of her parents' tolerance and ability to be considerate of other people's differences, writes also of the profound effect her sister's growing feminism had upon her, and of the support network that developed around her during her worst times of studying mechanics at technical college. Without those supports, she doubts she would have survived.

Here, history is again unkind to women: women's support networks are not a contemporary creation, though "networking" is promoted as though it has never been done before. Annmarie Turnbull speaks of the "important support network" amongst women on school boards in England from the 1870s. Writing of the period 1870 to 1904, Turnbull says that women "were frequently united [at that time] by their feminist and party politics, and also by close friendship":

Once members [of boards] themselves, women encouraged other women to stand. Alice Westlake and Helen Taylor suggested the idea to Rosamond Davenport-Hill and Elizabeth Garrett encouraged her sister Alice Cowell, Emily Davies and Rosamond Davenport-Hill to stand. Similar examples abound, and it is clear that throughout the 1870s and 1880s, and well into the 1890s this complex support network existed amongst the women members. They often argued, but their shared ideals meant that it was rare for a woman to attempt election without the support and encouragement of past or serving female members. In fact, so keen were the women members to ensure that their sex's interests would be represented on every board, that they trained possible successors before retiring from office . . .

Emily Davies noted bitterly after the defeat of the woman standing as her successor, that "It is vexing to have lost Greenwich. Isa worked hard . . ."[14]

Certainly networking amongst women is important for support, for passing information, for developing confidence in their own and other women's abilities. But it should not take upon itself the image of "never been done before", discounting the past efforts of women and the presently existing women's friendship networks of which Fiona Giles, Emel Corley, Jennifer Stott and the others write.

The fortune in the lining

Joan Mills doubted her own abilities for years — until she found her capacities were real. It was "like finding a fortune in the lining of an old coat". Mills was an adult before she made the discovery.[15] Young women should not have to grow older before they, too, come to this realisation. Jennifer Stott recognised that, as a *quid pro quo*, her journalist colleagues' support of her was matched by her presence having an effect on them — now, they take stories that previously "may never have got in". Mary Gartrell is not phased by having to stand up for her feminist ideals amongst her peers; she recognises her ability to do so with confidence. Sarah Gillman watched her grandmother's reawakening, upon the death of her husband (Sarah's grandfather), and they found support in each other's views and actions.

Women have been socialised into being dependent or, at least, recognising themselves in this way. The theme of dependency underlies their education at school — they are faced with a legacy of being channelled into areas where their vocations are classified as submissive, passive, dependent upon the roles and actions of others: they are persuaded to become secretaries, nurses, dental assistants. The executive — a man; the doctor — a man; the dentist — a man; all independent. Women are confined in librarianship or teaching to the lower rungs, answerable to a male boss. Women are taught they will be dependants in marriage (despite the reality of the very real work women do in keeping such relationships together). Women's abilities are downgraded or derided.

Yet, some women defy the image. Perhaps what they should be working to ensure is that the influences which are crucial to the feminism developing among some young women have an opportunity of extending to all young women. And that all young women, living under the umbrella of those influences, develop a strong recognition of their own ability to contribute. In 1851 Elizabeth Cady Stanton wrote in a letter to the Women's Rights Convention that:

> The girl must early be impressed with the idea that she is to be "a hand, not a mouth"; a worker, and not a drone, in the great hive of human activity.[16]

To grow up feminist, acknowledging the importance of the varying influences in one's life, and the effect that they have had upon one's life, is important; equally so, a young woman must grow up knowing she is an actor rather than an offsider in another actor's life. The walls of Elizabeth Cady Stanton's hive are being rushed — not one of these young women, growing up feminist, is a "drone"!

Jennifer Stott

Jennifer Stott, *twenty-one years of age at writing and a journalist working with a glossy women's fashion magazine in Sydney, was also a member of the Crystal Set women's radio collective.*
Photo courtesy of Candy Le Guay

I come from the heart of middle class, socially aspiring territory in Sydney, where I grew up with my three younger sisters and my parents. My high school years were spent at a private girls' school, bar time spent at the International School in Hamburg, West Germany, where my family lived for a year. Leaving school, I began work with a glossy women's magazine, with future hopes of entering the fashion industry. I began a degree in communications at the New South Wales Institute of Technology. Four years on, I have no desire now to enter the fashion industry.

Rather predictably, my family and upbringing have had an enormous effect on the moulding of my personality, and therefore on my feminism. My mother and I are very close. Often she acts as the conscience my brain doesn't have time to accommodate. Once, it frustrated me that her intelligence and strength seemed totally "wasted" or "misdirected". It remains a source of wonderment to me that in 1956 it wasn't really an issue to knock back a scholarship to university to work to save for a home.

My father is more open to feminism than I think he admits. In a marriage with a solid twenty-year history, his accommodation of changing roles and initiatives has been surprisingly positive. My three younger sisters are all strong achievers. The family unit has been taken as something "sacred" by those *in charge*, conducive to encouraging a false sense of dependency amongst us all, but also creating an environment of constant and intense interaction. The continual need to justify one's position on "anything" (largely for the sake of academic debate) means constant refining and reassessing of views. This has not meant everything about feminism has been wholeheartedly embraced; feminism has been subjected to the same rigorous questioning as anything else.

Doing my degree was when it all happened. My mind opened up. It did a bit of a shuffle. Several lecturers were influential in developing my position on feminism. One in particular personified my feminist ideals, was the subject of a variety of my emotions, ranging from adoration to obsession ... yes, I got over it eventually ...

Influences on me and my feminism have been numerous. Many more people and things have been important to me: I'm a bit of a bower bird; I collect bits of philosophy here, a quotation there, a little personality from that person, a mannerism from another. Whipping them together, I stir them into my own feminism. Two current influences on my perspective are the visit to Australia of British writer Beatrix Campbell, and Judith Allen's paper "Marxism and the Man Question" in *Beyond Marxism* — without too many qualms about the *slight* contradictions snuggled in there. Jeni Thornley's *Maidens* is a favourite film — no excuses, just cinematic seduction — and one of the very first feminist films I ever saw. It marks the beginning of a long involvement in questions surrounding women and the cinema and feminist film-making.

I consume tremendous amounts of literature. The brilliant *Serious Undertakings* by Helen Grace is one of the most important texts I've come across for ages, not only in terms of feminism ... Fran Lebowitz's *Metropolitan Life* perhaps applies — it showed me that humour was in fact possible; and it has made me want to live in New York.

And the work of the women's movement in the late 1960s and 1970s has influenced my consciousness and behaviour. It has meant that although society may continue to criticise choice of lifestyle and sexuality, a strong network of support reaffirms that you're not mad, not weird, not the only one. The women's movement has given us female role models, mentors, a network of alternative options.

With my writing, I have been fortunate. The senior people at work — the Editor in Chief and the Features Editor, in particular — have been extremely fair with me, offering invaluable advice and opportunities, tempering what are often wild fancies, and being very open to my ideas. A constant source of interest and the only writer I really "monitor" is Meaghan Morris, whose words can be found in both the most esoteric of journals and the mainstream press. Clever and witty, her writing manages to avoid that heavy-handed earnestness so often a symptom of the subjects she writes about.

Today, I am a full-time journalist in the mainstream media, writing primarily about the arts and "women's issues". Although working in a context that can foster anti-feminist ideas, my presence has effects. I will not write anything anti-feminist and stand (and can be heard) as a constant reminder of a feminist voice. Stories appear that may never have got a look in. For the most part, there is satisfaction in writing anything "new" for readers, whether about a form of theatre, or a progressive childcare conference. Only when I'm at my most desperate do I think that anything the mainstream touches turns to slick, losing its potency. Mostly, it's interesting and fun and you feel you're moving things.

The media has an enormous role to play in feminist struggles. Feminist media workers must challenge what is said, and the way it is said. In the past it's been too easy for the media (and then social and political structures) to pick up on women's liberation rhetoric and re-use it for their own ends. Gaining mainstream media attention is not the "be all". The alternative media is important. Crystal Set, the feminist radio programme on public broadcasting station 2SER-FM (108 on the dial) on Sundays from twelve noon to two p.m. offers the chance to experiment with how you're saying things as much as what you say. I've joined the Crystal Set collective, with ten other members, whose diversity indicates the range of issues covered on the show. It's a great collective — there's friendship, support, constructive criticism, and the sharing of knowledge and skills.

In the immediate future I suspect my work will be in the media. Journalism suits my aptitude for fossicking around, ferreting out interesting bits and pieces, mixing them into something else interesting. Yet needs and roles are always changing, so it's difficult to say where one is heading. There are some things I know: I don't like to sit still. That's one thing feminism has given me confidence to live out.

I attend various conferences and discussion groups, but working fulltime, being part of Crystal Set, and pursuing other interests like film and film studies, I don't have a great deal of "free" time. I don't believe in becoming involved in issues or collectives if I have no time or energy to offer them. I prefer to choose a couple of current interests and give them my best (even if those "current interests" change rapidly).

I have "career ambitions", but rather than seeing them in terms of a line upwards, I see a scribble all over the place. I like lots of different things at the one time. I'd hate to stagnate. Obviously mine is a privileged position — with the educational and employment opportunities to make such grand decisions about whether to go straight or to scribble. Many, in fact most, women do not.

Being able to make choices, feminism has allowed me to think seriously about work and priorities. It has freed me from constraints of ideologies like "Your work is your life" or "Your home is your life". Everything I do is a part of, but not my entire, existence. Something about not putting all your eggs . . . Some more fanciful ambitions are to study, live in New York, and retire in Venice at the age of thirty . . .

Motherhood interests me, but at this time seems invariably to beg the question "Why?" "Question your motives." Something Oriana Fallaci said in *Letter to a Child Never Born* strikes me as an apt answer: "To be a mother is not a trade, it's not even a duty. It's only one right among many." I would be having a child for *me*, but *also* for them.

My ideas about children are not conventional, but I certainly don't think they're selfish. I would hope my child would have strong relationships with many different people, right from the start, a position usually reserved only for parents. Somehow this seems to offer more scope in the role models chosen. Yet I do speak with great gusto from a pre-maternal position. All may change.

Marriage is not something I see myself involved with, for a number of reasons, not the least that I see the institution with little to offer other than a false sense of security. I am concerned about personal space. There's a niggling fear that intense relationships mean the loss of autonomy. But it's not something I lose a great deal of sleep over.

I devote all my energies to women, not only because it's more pleasurable and rewarding, but attempts to "convert men" always felt like you'd bashed your head against four walls before one door would open. Frankly, I am sick of men griping about feminists' protests, claiming they're general slurs on all men. Take rape, or domestic violence: "I wouldn't rape," they say, "I wouldn't bash my wife/lover/child." I'm sure most wouldn't, but it's time *they* started to organise. It's time they took some responsibility, and acted on feminist concerns.

Some issues that are important to me move outside feminism in one sense, but are also integrally linked in another. The anti-nuclear issue is one such case. Apart from what would happen if "they" dropped the bomb, some other areas are of concern. Women have worked in the peace movement for decades, but often for reasons clearly anti to many of the basic tenets of feminism. More recently, feminists have begun to grapple with the issue. Old stances such as "Women Know The Genesis of Life" or "We're Doing It For Our Babies" are being discussed and dealt with. We can say we're feminists and want peace. We want it for our children and our friends, but also for ourselves. Greenham Common is a unique protest by women: the weekend of Embrace The Base, where women joined hands around the nuclear weapons base in England, was a demonstration of women's power to protest in a way that could not be reacted against, and successfully turned public opinion in Britain around; now the majority of people are opposed to Cruise missiles. Yet the United States have still implemented their plans to deposit the missiles there.

Fuelling my anger against nuclear weapons is the massive

amount of money poured into the industry. I adhere to Baudrillard's notion that it is not the nuclear war that's the horror,
it's the threat:

> It isn't that the direct menace of atomic destruction
> paralyses our lives. It is rather that deterrence leukomizes
> us. And this deterrence comes from a situation which
> excludes the real atomic clash.

> J. Baudrillard,
> *The Precession of Simulacra*

Although this takes Baudrillard right out of the context of
some of his other ideas, it is worth thinking about. Perhaps it
points to the stupidity of the amount of money spent on the
nuclear arms race, when it (not to mention mega-politics)
could be seen as such a farce.

Feminist action now takes on the conservative movement bred
during our economically recessive period. Women began
asking for jobs when they were being denied in increasing
numbers to all. But women have as much right to paid
employment as anyone, and an important role to play in
economic recovery. It's important for women to have money.
Money seems to be the proverbial root of most things, and
there's nothing like a bit of poverty for fostering the appeal of
pregnancy and marriage, complete with their false sense of
security. I hope for a society beyond one based on money, but
in the present the unfair distribution of wealth and income
must be changed.

There are serious dangers in the creation of a massive
welfare state. But lack of money breeds demoralisation and
physical and emotional oppression. Redistribution through the
welfare system is one method, not to be used alone, but to be
used in conjunction with other ways of redistributing wealth,
money, and power.

Battles must still be fought to counter the double load of
work for women. A premise on which men fought for the
thirty-five hour week was that of more leisure time. What of
more time to spend at home sharing in domestic labour? What
also of more efforts and more energy by men as well as women
on the question of adequate childcare?

Today, insidious tactics are being used to undermine the

strength and solidarity of the women's movement. This is nothing new. A decade ago feminism was attacked as "counter-nature". But now, the media constantly depicts women as "already liberated". This invites feelings of insecurity and inadequacy in women who are not able to fulfil an impossible image. Now we have a situation where women can have it all — they can fuck as much as they like (they've got the Pill), work a forty hour week (they wanted "equality"), and children and a home (they couldn't bear to part with that part of life they do so well). What do men get out of this? More fucks, less pressure on their earning capacity and the same free domestic labour. What do women get? A nervous breakdown.

Reinforcing the "failings" of feminism on a "philosophical" level, we find a spate of stories in the media dealing with the "post-feminist generation" (sic). As I understand it from the women who have been in the feminist movement for many years, there have always been differences and divisions because of class, race, and the like, but this hasn't stopped women working together. Media stories work on divisions in the women's movement, highlighting differences and positing them as a new phenomenon. It's just a different sort of attack. Maybe it's a testament to the strength of the women's movement and its threat to the existing structure that such a response is felt to be necessary.

As for me, as both a feminist and a twenty-one-year old, I should fall into what is described as the "second generation" of the new women's movement. But there's no generation gap here. I am never really conscious of any age differences of women I'm involved with. Some of the most pressing issues facing feminists have changed, perhaps — but I'm in there with my sisters, younger, older, my age, pulling at the oars.

Fiona Giles

Fiona Giles, *born on 9 July 1958 in Perth, Western Australia, is a member of many organisations, including the Federated Clerks' Union and the Australian Labor Party. When she wrote her piece, she was a Women's Department worker with the Australian Union of Students in Melbourne.*

For many years I avoided using the term feminist to describe myself, much as I avoided other political and personal labels. At the age of twenty-four my position has changed and I am happy to identify myself as a feminist, defend feminist aims and support other women. However, I remain sympathetic to my earlier squeamishness and would like to outline my reasons for it. At the same time I hope to show how my political views and their "crookedness" can be justified and, perhaps, be politically useful.

While I now accept a political appellation, membership of a political (Labor) party, and a political responsibility, my direction both professionally and personally is away from politics. Instead, I would prefer to take a political conscious-ness out of the fray and use it to colour any other activity I might take up. This means that I experience a continual strain between political commitment and the desire for an occupation outside of "political" institutions. For while accepting that everything is political — that all statements and action can be ideologically categorised and have political consequences — I do not accept that politics is everything.

One of the characteristics of feminism is that it is essentially diffuse. Yet feminists are commonly considered as extreme monotypes (through, among other things, the popular media use of the "dragon" caricature). Because of this I feel that spreading contagious, even subversive, images of feminism and communicating feminist values through subterfuge is often just as helpful as becoming a "femocrat" or a separatist. For although women could theoretically be organised by feminism into a huge interest group based simply on gender, there are greater concerns of humanity in general which must go far beyond feminism. Women must address these concerns as well as the principal and immediate female concerns if we are to avoid becoming guardians of "feminist" values in the same way as women were previously thought to be guardians of "feminine" values. Defending the equality and rights of women must remain a central objective, but defending the equality of people and the very existence of humanity is just as, if not more, important. Consequently, I value the multifarious nature of feminism: its ability to permeate all organised and disorganised efforts to change.

Another problem faced by the feminist movement today is that the relevance of feminism to young women is not immediately evident — even to young women who are familiar with its ideas and objectives. Nor are the values of feminism particularly attractive to young women who are already convinced that they can do anything. Ironically, this comfortable condition was made possible by feminist campaigns, for feminism has always contended that women can in fact do more than they were led to believe. However, the puritanical zeal with which feminists often reject dominant feminine images is, it seems, continually alienating to young heterosexual women. While the task of providing a third alternative set of options for young women's self-regard and fashion is extremely difficult (particularly in the face of hostile mass media), it is a sign of failure that the traditional images are still, to many, preferable to the left-wing alternative.

Feminism must be inclusive; it wasn't in the 1970s when women were still defining their alternative to patriarchal definitions, but seems to be becoming more so now. As a reformist movement feminism is perhaps doomed to disappear and reappear, as cycles of capitalist production draw women into the paid workforce and force them out again. And like motherhood — the tragic profession — the sign of a reformist movement being successful is that it is no longer needed. Feminism is still needed; but not in the same ways, by the same people.

I was born in Perth in 1958, into a politically aware family which, as a family, changed dramatically at certain stages, as my mother changed, and as western society charted its way through the self-appraising 1970s. My introduction to feminism coincided with my mother's growing socialist and feminist awareness and commitment. My feminism was not based on personal experience so much as on an abstract belief in equality, and was a response to observed inequality. As my mother began to express her disaffection with marriage I was becoming articulate, interested in ideas for their own sake, and concerned with my own need to account for the differences between my potential and my desires.

I was not a radical feminist at any stage, although I sympathise with the need for separation. At times I was hardly feminist at all and often rebelled against what seemed to be a family orthodoxy. But while my views are and were undoubtedly more equivocal than those of my feminist siblings and mother, I recognise that I have benefited enormously from my feminist background. It is feminism (as well as the left-wing liberal environment in which I was brought up) which equipped me with my critical fighting faculties.

In addition, although I may contest many of the finer points of feminist thought, I do not oppose the basic principles of feminism. I believe that all women and men should have equal entitlements; and generally they do not. But I have doubts about the belief, for example, that women can change themselves at will, through heightened "self-awareness".

If I have any advantage of time over older feminists it would be through being an adolescent in the 1970s. At a time which for me entailed natural and inevitable change, everyone of all ages seemed to be changing. As sexual relations were increasingly being analysed as a social manifestation of power, I was discovering sex. As women were reappraising their roles and ambitions, I was beginning seriously to formulate my own for the first time. And as the general populace was taking to the street in demonstrations of political discontent, I was becoming old enough to march and to express my own political opinions. Being younger, I was allowed to watch the foibles of others without having to join in, either personally or political-ly. I was permitted to have a choice seat looking on, but not expected to involve myself in the transitions of people around me. While not being expected to cut off my hair or to leave a husband, I was able to observe the many conflicts and comfort the casualties. I witnessed a great deal of turmoil, naturally failing to escape some of my own. But I was happily in a position to make judgements without having to take sides.

Fourth born into a family of five children, I was nurtured on ideas by my communist-atheist father. We fostered a labour-oriented yet individualist ideology well suited to the new femin-ism that was about to arise, and to the dissolution of the family itself. Ideas originating in the family as sophisticated "dinner party" insights eventually became views which were lived, breathed and enacted as an all-consuming occupation.

My father's one-time communist views reinforced his belief in the virtue of hard work and the natural justice of achieve-ment. No comforts, he believed, were, or should be, inherit-able. My mother, coming from a slightly different Protestant background and the female class where success is more problematic, also believed in the value of hard work, although she was not so secure in the belief that hard work necessarily sufficed advancement, and was consequently less interested in competition for its own sake. Both my parents believed in the intrinsic value of education. They particularly valued state education as a universal right, and as a means of creating a more equal society. In addition, they made no apparent discrimination between us concerning our abilities for, or rights to, such an education. Although they would have reconciled themselves to a family "dropout", the professed utility and advantage of a comprehensive education which would "keep the options open" was too well argued for any of us to resist.

My childhood was dominated by the values of my father. My mother supported the family and property, while my father worked (extremely hard) as a medical practitioner. My mother resigned her nursing position soon after marriage and devoted herself to maintaining a large house and family, while also being involved in parent and teacher organisations and other community welfare groups.

During my teenage years the values and activities of my mother became more dominant in my life, and my allegiance was to her on the whole. My father continued to work long hours and looked towards a stable — but unstable — domestic background for support. My mother matriculated as a mature-aged student and attended university. She stood for Parliament and local government as an independent candidate, took out a Bachelor of Arts degree in politics, entered the workforce and became a public figure.

We were a reasonably affluent family, and while getting most that we asked for as children, were expected to achieve great things in return. This background of just deserts was probably as strong a motivating force during my teenage years, and is now, as any feminist sense of entitlement. As children we were encouraged to be ambitious, critical and enquiring. We were also led to believe, however, that the laureates offered from time to time by society (however imperfect that society might be) were worth striving for. This assumption was later questioned when it seemed that the price of achievement for women was eternal compromise, and resulted for me in a wavering tendency to succeed and to reject. On a more day-to-day level, I emulated the strength and competence of my older brother and sisters. My sisters tried to keep me in line morally (directing me never to repeat dirty jokes or to behave like a lesbian). My brother set the physical standards. The most humiliating insult he could use against me was that I was a "feeble female". This taunted me greatly and I spent years of manly outdoors activities hoping to overcome my apparent female limitations. Similarly, my peers at school valued physical achievement and moral conformity over originality, intelligence and affection. In such a context, the values of feminism came to a jaded thirteen-year-old like the flowers of September.

Discrimination did exist, both latently and otherwise, throughout my childhood. But this was not oppressively felt at any stage within the family. Instead, the dominant values of the family were ones of competence, tenacity and a willingness to experiment. Cuteness and beguiling stupidity were tolerated but not encouraged. It was at high school that gender-based injustices became evident, both within the structure of the school and from the — again moral — expectations of my peers. By then, however, I was equipped more or less to cope with the obstacles of sexism, or at least to see them as simply that. More importantly, my mother changed as I did. And as the independence, both economic and personal, of the various members of the family forced it to disband, I became more independent too. Our version of the nuclear family, as an economic institution, self-destructed and became obsolete to most of us. So at sixteen I left home, taking a feminist advantage with me in the form of the elusive "freedom to choose". Now, at twenty-four, I'm much younger, and prepared to push and slide with the rest, to a certain extent.

I couldn't say that I didn't experience sexism within the family as a child. But I don't recall any grave injustices perpetrated simply through being a girl. And I doubt that any particular childhood incident motivated my interest in feminism — which was more of an intellectual adventure than the results of an unlocked store of thwarted hopes. Similarly, I have firmer childhood memories of wanting a profession than of wanting a marriage. I thought about marriage as a child and entertained myself with domestic games. But the image of myself in a white laboratory coat tinkering with instruments under gleaming lights (I was intent, most unrealistically, on becoming a scientist) was certainly clearer and more alluring than the one created by Mum's net curtains wrapped toga-wise around my too-flat body for the purposes of bridal transformation.

My central feminist views, when I first became interested in the early 1970s, concerned the politics of housework and motherhood, the related ideology of the family, and sexual freedom. I read *The Female Eunuch* in 1972 and wrote a high school essay on the housewife's syndrome in 1974. For English classes I wrote about the material bases of the nuclear family and about intense and convoluted personal and social relations, most often hoping to argue the need for community responsibility. At the same time I was reading widely in general, and I must admit to being just as influenced by the ideas of Camus, de Beauvoir, Miller, Nin and others between the years 1974 and 1977. I was particularly attracted to the stance of the French existentialists (this seemed to be the fashion) which conveniently accommodated notions of control of the self in the context of absurdity and general human decline. There was nothing to lose and heaps to gain if your tastes were sordid enough. However, I have also maintained a feminist interest in my studies and wrote my honours thesis on the feminist fiction of Margaret Drabble. I was attracted to the style of Germaine Greer, her flamboyance, apparent erudition and eloquence. I viewed the work of Elizabeth Reid with admiration and, at seventeen, paid close attention (aided by my mother's participation) to the activities, aims and conference of International Women's Year. Of women who have personally affected me, Irene Greenwood, whom I came to know at about the same time, must rate as one of the most interesting. She is not only a continuing good friend but a great reminder of the importance of the past to the women's movement, and the value of women's history. While offering me an insight into some of the values of age for us all, Irene also gave me an idea of the many women who have campaigned all their lives throughout this century and long before feminism became even remotely fashionable.

I attended the first Women's Liberation Meeting in Perth in 1972 and remember both resenting and being amused by the male interjectors who persistently tried to steer the discussion towards the subject of superfluous facial hair and why men shouldn't shave if women weren't intending to. It was a typical meeting for me to attend at the time, as I also helped out — as we all did — with my mother's election campaigns, and generally sought to be "involved". (This passed.) I suspect I was a bit blasé about women organising for the first time, given that my own feminist interest was more detached and less urgent than the older women's. But I was genuinely interested in the aims of women's liberation and in the sentiments of socialism, democratic accountability, the community values of education and many other hopes for perfectibility which were current at the time. I marched in moratorium marches throughout the early 1970s, attended peace rallies and listened to Whitlam and Hawke holding forth while becoming increasingly sceptical about their claims and wondering what they intended doing for Aborigines, women and trees, not to mention the world economic order. I attended meetings of the Secondary Students' Union and went on strike for a day to support student participation in education policy, abolish corporal punishment, reform the narrow academic bias of curriculum, and all that.

In 1972, equipped with a letter from the then Director-

General of Education regarding the right of students not to wear uniforms, I refused to wear my outdated school tunic to school. I encouraged enough of my girlfriends to see the sense of not wearing a dress in winter and to support the cause by wearing jeans, in a wanton "flouting of authority", as the irate headmistress put it. It was a triumphant campaign, revolution-ising (as only could be done in the early seventies) our attitudes to school authority, leading to the introduction of trousers for schoolgirls and to a much more rational attitude to uniforms generally. It was an important incident for me in testing my fighting power as a fourteen-year-old and it probably represents the beginning and end of my brilliant political career as I've known it.

My occasional rebellion against feminism and its assumptions has appeared in a variety of ways over the years. It has involved a refusal to appear as a feminist should, a refusal to behave on militant or "educational" lines with regard to male friends, or sometimes simply to make feminist generalisations. More recently, I have been sceptical of the feminist intent to defy or suppress our individual pasts so as to be more ideologically sound. And when faced with the associated theories concern-ing the value of consciousness-raising I can only say that, in such a context, I would prefer my own (over) consciousness to be razed.

At home I was certainly the corrupt weak link, refusing to purchase or sell any wholesale dogma. (At school I must have been nevertheless seen as hopelessly radical.) The motives were partly personal (I wanted to be free to experiment and make my own mistakes, and judge my own day-to-day circum-stances), partly perverse (I wanted to be different), and partly based on a genuine conviction that some feminist beliefs were mistaken. I was also more attracted to fulfilling my own curiosity about life than devoting my time to politics and the eternal task of persuasion. Perhaps this is why I am now happy to rationalise my differences as differences of style and occupation rather than allegiance.

I would like to marry one day, I think. The main problem is to include everything else I want to do. But I'm willing to try. I feel that marriage as a contract is certainly imperfect and based on requirements of property ownership rather than the needs of individuals. My own property requirements are such that marriage is perhaps unnecessary. But it could still be a nice community affirmation of a partnership. Partnership is another problem.

I would like to have children and I am committed to the provision of childcare so that everyone who wishes to can do so while maintaining their economic independence or simply occupying themselves in other ways. I do not think much of the nuclear family as a means of organising society. I would prefer to live in a society where the burden and joys of childrearing are more equitably shared.

I would like men to be sufficiently different (although I could not say whether the change would be achieved through conditioning, re-education or mind-altering chemicals) so that they would be less violent and less egocentric. I don't particularly want men to be more sympathetic or even more feminist, but I would prefer them, among other things, to be less predatory. I would like to feel safer at night and to go as I please without having to rely on men for protection from other men.

I wish we could find some way of learning from history, so as not endlessly to repeat mistakes while getting better at making the effects of those mistakes more far-reaching. And I wouldn't mind living to a grand old age. I've a feeling that life gets better for women with time, as less is expected of them, eccentricity is tolerated, and children come and go.

CHAPTER SIX

Epilogue

. . . we have to learn to live now the future we are fighting for, rather than compromising in vain hope of a future that is always deferred, always unreal. This creative leap implies a kind of recklessness born out of the death of false hope.

Mary Daly,
Beyond God the Father, 1973

At regular intervals throughout women's history, the claim has been made that feminism is dead.[1] The cry is uttered too soon. Whether the older women in today's movement continue to dwell upon the lack of young women in their organisations or not, young women will flock to their own brand of feminism. Cathy Henry is not currently involved in any organised women's group, but she describes herself as a feminist and lives according to her principles. Jennifer Stott doesn't believe in the charge that she is part of a post-feminist generation. Why should she indeed? She is part of a feminist generation, which she sees as unbounded by age. To Cathy Henry, there is a generation gap in the membership of women's organisations like the Women's Electoral Lobby, but that does not impede her feminism. Sarah Gillman believes that feminism should not be bound by "images and technicalities". She defines herself as feminist. Similarly, Fiona Giles has "often rebelled against what seemed to be a family orthodoxy". Diana Forward is "slightly hostile towards organised feminist groups". Karen Ermacora has only recently become aware of feminism. Mary Gartrell includes in her circle of friends both feminists and those who do not subscribe to the belief. Like Emel Corley, Michele Trewick and Anna Donald, each of them is a feminist.

And importantly, within the range of their concerns and their belief that women have a right to be equal in the present world, not in some far-off future, they include a true commitment to the class struggle, the conservation movement, the rights of black Australians to live free of racism, and the elimination of war. Peace is central to their activism and their labouring to achieve a feminist world.

Each of these young women — who is replicated in every community, in every country town, every state throughout Australia — recognises also the need for boys and men to change in order that feminism may come into its own. As Fiona Giles writes, "I would like men to be sufficiently different . . ." Each of these young women — and her counterparts — is courageous in adopting a style of living which incorporates such demands. It is a courage Adrienne Rich has recognised:

> If I could have one wish for my own sons, it is that they should have the courage of women. I mean by this something very concrete and precise; the courage I have seen in women who, in their private and public lives, both in the interior world of their dreaming, thinking, and creating, and the outer world of patriarchy, are taking greater and greater risks, both psychic and physical, in the evolution of a new vision.[2]

The victory is conceivable. Courage has its own momentum. In the words of Millicent Garrett Fawcett: "Courage calls to courage everywhere, and its voice cannot be denied."[3]

Endnotes

Chapter one **Education**

1. A.G. Austin, *Australian Education 1788-1900: Church, State and Public Education in Colonial Australia*, 3rd edn, Pitman, Carlton, 1972, p. 72.
2. Paige Porter, "Social Policy, Education and Women in Australia", in Baldock and Cass (eds), *Women, Social Welfare and the State*, George Allen and Unwin, Sydney, 1983, pp. 247-8.
3. M. Hutton Neve, *This Mad Folly: A History of Australian Pioneer Women Doctors*, Library of Australian History, Sydney, 1980.
4. ibid.
5. Bek McPaul, "A Woman Pioneer", *Australian Law Journal* 22, 1948, p. 2.
6. See for example, Michelle Stanworth, *Gender and Schooling: A Study of Sexual Divisions in the Classroom*, Women's Research and Resources Centre Publication, London, 1981; Susan Cosgrove, "Do You Discriminate Against Girls in Your Classroom?", *SASTA*, December 1981; Carolyn Ingvarson and Anne Jones, "Sexism in Science", *SASTA*, December 1981; Dale Spender, *Invisible Women — The Schooling Scandal*, Routledge Keegan Paul, London, 1982.
7. Ingvarson and Jones, op. cit. (note 6), p. 22.
8. See generally discussion in Lois Wladis Hoffman, "Early Childhood Experiences and Women's Achievement Motives", in Mednick, Tangri and Hoffman (eds), *Women and Achievement — Social and Motivational Analyses*, Halstead Press/John Wiley and Sons, New York, 1975, p. 129; Aletha H. Stein and Margaret M. Bailey, "The Socialization of Achievement Motivation in Females", in Mednick, Tangra and Hoffman, ibid., p. 151; Irene Hanson Frieze, "Women's Expectations for and Causal Attributions of Success and Failure", in Mednick, Tangri and Hoffman, ibid., p. 158.
9. ibid.
10. Ingvarson and Jones, op. cit. (note 6), p. 21; Spender, op. cit. (note 6).
11. See for example, Alison Kelly (ed.), *The Missing Half — Girls and Science Education*, Manchester University Press, 1981;

Lynn H. Fox, Linda Brody and Dianne Tobin (eds), *Women and the Mathematical Mystique*, Johns Hopkins University Press, Baltimore, 1980; also Ingvarson and Jones, op. cit. (note 6), p. 21; Victoria Foster, *Changing Choices: Girls, School and Work*, Hale and Iremonger, Sydney, 1984.

12. Spender, op. cit. (note 6), Chapter 6, "Girls — Being Negative for Boys", pp. 77ff.
13. Dorothy Smith, "A Peculiar Eclipsing: Women's Exclusion from Man's Culture", *Women's Studies International Quarterly*, 1 (No. 4), p. 287.
14. Spender, op. cit. (note 6), pp. 39-40.
15. This is obvious in other areas, for example law. See Jocelynne A. Scutt, "Sexism in Criminal Law", in Mukherjee and Scutt (eds), *Women and Crime*, George Allen and Unwin, Sydney, 1980.
16. Spender, op. cit. (note 6), pp. 41-2.
17. Millicent Poole, *Youth — Expectations and Transitions*, London, 1983, pp. 134-268, 271.
18. Hoffman, op. cit. (note 8), p. 134 et. seq.
19. Department of Education and Youth Affairs, *Funding Guidelines to the Commonwealth Education Commissions for 1984*, AGPS, Canberra, 1984.
20. Cosgrove, op. cit. (note 6), p. 11.
21. Ingvarson and Jones, op. cit. (note 6), p. 23.
22. Lynne Symons, "Elimination of Waste is a Total Asset", *SASTA*, December 1981.
23. Barbara Small and Judith Whyte, "Girls into Science and Technology: The First Two Years", *SASTA*, December 1981, pp. 9-10.

Chapter two **Employment**

1. The documentary film *Rosie the Riviter* shows this occurring during the second World War and its aftermath in the United States; similarly in Australia, the film *For Love or Money* gives an Australian perspective on the issue. See Megan McMurchy, Margot Oliver and Jeni Thornley, *For Love or Money — A Pictorial History of Women and Work in Australia*, Penguin Books Australia, Ringwood, 1983; also Carmel Shute, "From Balaclavas to Bayonets: Women's Voluntary War Work, 1939-41", *Hecate*, VI (No. 1), 1980; Lynne Beaton, "The Importance of Women's Paid Labour — Based on the Study of Women at Work in the Second World War", in Convenors (eds), *Second Women and Labour Conference Papers*, Melbourne, 1980.
2. See for example, "The Suitability of Pit-Brow Work",

Englishwoman's Review, February 1886; reprinted in Janet Horowitz Murray (ed.) *Strong-Minded Women — And Other Lost Voices from 19th-century England*, Penguin Books, Harmondsworth, 1984, p. 374; Anthony Ashley Cooper, Lord Ashley, "Speech on the Ten Hours Bill (1884)", *Hansard (UK)*, House of Commons, 15 March 1844; reprinted in Murray, ibid., p. 341.

3. Per Lord Neaves in *Jex-Blake* v. *Senatus of the University of Edinburgh* (1873) 11 M. 784.

4. Published in full in *In re Edith Haynes* (1904) 6 WAR 209, pp. 213-14.

5. Per Burnside J. in *In re Edith Haynes* (1904) 6 WAR 209, p. 214. The judge's research abilities were somewhat lacking: in 1873 in the United States Myra Bradwell had in fact applied for admission to the Bar of Illinois. See *Bradwell* v. *Illinois* (1873) 83 US 130.

6. *In re Kitson* (1920) SALR 230

7. *Ex parte Ogden* (1893) 16 NSW LR 86.

8. See discussion in Jocelynne A. Scutt, "Legislating for the Right to be Equal", in Cora V. Baldock and Bettina Cass (eds), *Women, Social Welfare and the State*, George Allen and Unwin, Sydney, 1983, p. 223; also J. Mackinolty, "To Stay or to Go — Sacking Married Women Teachers" in J. Mackinolty and H. Radi (eds), *In Pursuit of Justice: Australian Women and the Law 1788-1979*, Hale and Iremonger, Sydney, 1979, p. 140. In the United Kingdom laws were similarly passed: see Alison M. Oram, "Serving Two Masters? The Introduction of a Marriage Bar in Teaching in the 1920s", in London Feminist History Group (eds), *Men's Power, Women's Resistance — The Sexual Dynamics of History*, Pluto Press, London, 1983, p. 134.

9. See discussion, Jocelynne A. Scutt, "A Time for Action — Education, Employment and Australian Women", in Maria de Leo and Michele Salmon (eds), *1980: A New ERA for Women — The WEL Papers*, WEL (Victoria), Melbourne, 1980, p. 29; also, *New South Wales' Government Review of Administration* ("Wilenski Report"), Government Printer, Sydney, 1979; Chloe Refshauge, "Bearers of Burdens: Occupational Safety without Discrimination", in Third Women and Labour Conference Collective, (eds), *Working it Out — All Her Labours*, Hale and Iremonger, Sydney, 1984, p. 70.

10. Wilenski Report, op. cit., p. 199.

11. *NSW Receptionist Course Manual*, Public Service Board.

12. Cecelia Clarke, Eileen Mason, Edna Ryan and Jocelynne A. Scutt, *WEL Submission to the National Wage Case 1983*, Sydney/Melbourne, 1983.

13. ibid.

14. Margaret Thornton, "(Un)equal Pay for Work of Equal Value", in *Journal of Industrial Relations*, (No. 4), December 1981.
15. Clarke, Mason, Ryan and Scutt, op. cit. See also *National Wage Case*, Melbourne, 23 September 1983, in the Australian Conciliation and Arbitration Commission, Reasons for Decision.
16. See for example, Kay Hargreaves, *Women at Work*, Penguin Books, Ringwood, 1982; Chris Ronalds, *Anti-Discrimination Legislation in Australia*, Butterworths, Sydney, 1979; Chris Ronalds, "To Right a Few Wrongs: Legislation Against Sex Discrimination", in Mackinolty and Radi, op. cit. (note 8), p. 190; Jocelynne A. Scutt, "Legislating for the Right to be Equal", in Baldock and Cass, op. cit. (note 8).
17. Keith Windshuttle, "Where John Stone has gone wrong", in *The National Times*, August 31-September 6 1984, p.18.
18. Ann Game and Rosemary Pringle, *Gender at Work*, George Allen and Unwin, Sydney, 1983.
19. ibid.
20. Cynthia Cockburn, *Brothers — Male Dominance and Technological Change*, Pluto Press, London, 1983.
21. ibid.
22. See Greg McGregor, "The dream houses of Christine Vadasz", in *The National Times*, March 9-15 1984, p.17.
23. Reported upon at the Australian Institute of Political Science seminar, "Women and the Bureaucracy", Sydney, April 1983.
24. See generally NSW Government Review of Administration, *Affirmative Action Handbook*, Government Printer, Sydney, 1979.

Chapter three Marriage

1. *Di divortio Lotharii et Tetbergae*, cited Jo-Ann McNamara and Suzanne F. Wemple, "Marriage and Divorce in the Frankish Kingdom", in Susan Mosher Stuard (ed.), *Women in Medieval Society*, University of Pennsylvania Press, 1976, p. 108.
2. Susan Mosher Stuard, "Women in Charter and Statute Law", in Stuard, op. cit., p. 201.
3. ibid., p. 204.
4. ibid.
5. "The Good Wife", extract from *The Goodman of Paris*; republished in James Bruce Ross and Mary Martin McLaughlin (eds), *The Portable Medieval Reader*, Penguin Books, Harmondsworth, 1977, pp. 154-5.
6. ibid., pp. 155-6.
7. ibid., pp. 156-9. (Compare this with the more modern approach of *The Australian Women's Weekly* and similar magazines — there is little difference!)

8. Caroline Norton, *English Laws for Women in the Nineteenth Century*, London, 1854; republished as *Caroline Norton's Defense — English Laws for Women in the Nineteenth Century*, Academy Chicago, Illinois, 1982, particularly pp. 17-18. For a more detailed discussion of the law of marriage and women's position during the nineteenth and early twentieth centuries, see Jocelynne A. Scutt, *Even in the Best of Homes — Violence in the Family*, Penguin Books, Ringwood, 1983, Chapter 2; Jocelynne A. Scutt and Di Graham, *For Richer, For Poorer — Money, Marriage and Property Rights*, Penguin Books, Ringwood, 1984, Chapter 4.

9. See discussion in Scutt, *Even in the Best of Homes*, op. cit.

10. See Roderick Phillips, *Divorce in New Zealand: A Social History*, Oxford University Press, Auckland, 1981; also, Scutt, *Even in the Best of Homes*, op. cit. (note 8).

11. See Scutt and Graham, *For Richer, For Poorer*, op. cit. (note 8).

12. Lincoln Day, "An Overview of the Australian Family Today", in Jocelynne A. Scutt (ed.), *Violence in the Family*, Australian Institute of Criminology, Canberra, 1980.

13. See Scutt, *Even in the Best of Homes*, op. cit. (note 8), particularly Chapter 9.

14. Faye Fransella and Kay Frost, *How Women See Themselves*, Tavistock Publications, London, 1977.

15. See for example, Dorothy Dinnerstein, *The Rocking of the Cradle — The Ruling of the World*, Souvenir Press, New York, 1976.

16. Women's Bureau, Department of Employment and Industrial Relations, *Facts on Women at Work in Australia 1982*, AGPS, Canberra, 1983.

17. New South Wales Anti-Discrimination Board, *Report*, Government Printer, Sydney, 1983.

18. For a review of the cases, see Jocelynne A. Scutt, "Principle v. Practice: Defining 'Equality' in Family Property Division on Divorce" (1983) 57 ALJ 143; also Scutt and Graham, *For Richer, For Poorer*, op. cit. (note 8).

19. See generally, Rebecca Bailey, "De Factos, Property and the Law" (1979) 52 ALJ 174; New South Wales Law Reform Commission, *Report on De Facto Relationships*, Government Printer, Sydney, 1982.

20. *Allen* v. *Snyder* (1977) 2 NSW LR 685.

21. Unreported, New South Wales Supreme Court, Court of Appeal, 23 August 1982, No. 115 of 1981.

22. On equal rights to marital assets and the need to change the *Family Law Act* 1975 (Cth) and the *Marriage Act* 1961 (Cth) to accommodate this system — at least for married and de facto

couples — see Scutt and Graham, *For Richer, For Poorer*, op. cit. (note 8).

23. For example, New South Wales — *Anti-Discrimination Act 1977*; Victoria — Equal Opportunity Bill 1984 (the Act was finally passed without the provisions relating to private life).

Chapter four **Children**

1. On marriage and children generally, see Diana Leonard Barker, "The Regulation of Marriage: Repressive Benevolence", in Garry Littlejohn, Barry Smart, John Wakeford and Nira Yuvia-Davis (eds), *Power and the State*, Croom Helm, London, 1978.

2. The words of a male anthropologist from the United Kingdom of Pacific Islanders, cited in Evelyn Reed, *Women's Evolution — From Matriarchal Clan to Patriarchal Family*, Pathfinder Press, New York, 1975.

3. See Evelyn Reed, ibid.

4. Article in *New Law Journal;* copy held by author.

5. Caroline Norton, *English Laws for Women in the Nineteenth Century*, London, 1854; republished as *Caroline Norton's Defense — English Laws for Women in the Nineteenth Century*, Academy Chicago, Illinois, 1982. The following quotation also comes from this source.

6. Elizabeth Badinter, *The Myth of Motherhood — An Historical View of the Motherhood Instinct*, Condor/Souvenir Press (E & A) Ltd, USA, 1981.

7. See Judith Allen, *Octavus Beal Reconsidered*, in Sydney History Group (eds), *What Rough Beast?*, George Allen and Unwin, Sydney, 1982.

8. See Barbara A. Hanawalt, "Women Before the Law: Females as Felons and Prey in Fourteenth-Century England", in D. Kelly Weisberg (ed.), *Women and the Law — The Social Historical Perspective*, vol. 1, Schenkman Publishing Company, Inc., Massachusetts, 1982; J. M. Beattie, "The Criminality of Women in Eighteenth-Century England" in Weisberg, ibid.

9. Some documents from the Commission are published in Ruth Teale, *Colonial Eve — Sources on Women in Australia 1788-1919*, Oxford University Press, Melbourne, 1978; also Beverly Kingston, *The World Moves Slowly*, Cassell Australia, Sydney, 1977.

10. ibid.

11. ibid.

12. See Faye Fransella and Kay Frost, *How Women See Themselves*, Tavistock Publications, London, 1977.

13. ibid.

14. ibid.

15. Lincoln Day, "An Overview of the Australian Family Today", in Jocelynne A. Scutt (ed.), *Violence in the Family*, Australian Institute of Criminology, Canberra, 1980.

16. ibid.

17. Nancy Romer, *The Sex Role Cycle: Socialisation from Infancy to Old Age*, Feminist Press/McGraw Hill, New York, 1981.

18. ibid.

19. Cited in Fransella and Frost, op. cit. (note 12).

20. See studies cited in Fransella and Frost, op. cit. (note 12).

21. For a comprehensive account and refutation of these studies, see Jocelynne A. Scutt, "The Politics of the 'Broken Home' in the Determination of Female Criminality", *Australian Quarterly*, 49, 1977.

22. See Fransella and Frost, op. cit. (note 12).

23. See Ann Oakley, *Housewife*, Penguin, Harmondsworth, 1976; see also Romer, op. cit. (note 17).

24. See Oakley, ibid., and Romer, op. cit. (note 17). See also Graeme Russell, *The Changing Role of Fathers?*, University of Queensland Press, Brisbane, 1983.

25. See "The Tax-Transfer System and the Family", in Maria de Leo and Michele Salmon (eds), *1980: A New ERA for Women — The WEL papers*, Melbourne, 1980, p. 19; also "Policy for Parents" in *1980 WEL Papers*, p. 22.

26. See Russell, op. cit. (note 24).

27. Attorney-General's Department (Cth), *Report on Maintenance Arrangements*, Canberra, ACT, 1984.

28. ibid.

29. Press report on the release of the Attorney-General's report, op. cit. (note 27).

30. "Lesbian Motherhood", in *ISIS — Women's International Information and Communication Service*, June 1982, p. 22.

31. *In the Marriage of N. and N.* (1977) FLC ¶ 90-208, 76,078, at 76,079.

32. *In the Marriage of Spry and Spry* (1977) FAC ¶ 90-271, 76,441, at 76,445.

33. *In the Marriage of Cartwright and Cartwright* (1977) FLC ¶ 90-302, 76,595, at 76,600.

34. ibid.

35. See Dorothy Dinnerstein, *The Rocking of the Cradle — The Ruling of the World*, Souvenir Press, New York, 1976; Dorothy Dinnerstein, *The Mermaid and the Minotaur*, University of California Press, Berkeley, California, 1976; Nancy Chodorow, *Reproduction of Mothering*, University of California Press, Berkeley, California, 1978.

36. Lee Mackay, "Developing an Alternative to the Nuclear Family", in *ISIS — Women's International Information and Communication Service*, June 1982, p. 29.
37. Some moves are being made in this area — slowly. Both the New South Wales and Victorian Departments of Education have formulated rules which allow a woman teacher to return to the service after a year's maternity leave at the level she would have attained had she not taken leave.

Chapter five **Influences**

1. Dale Spender, *There's Always Been a Women's Movement this Century*, Pandora Press, London, 1983; and see Mary Stott, *Forgetting's No Excuse — The Autobiography of Mary Stott, Journalist, Campaigner and Feminist*, Virago/Quartet Books, London, 1975.
2. Dale Spender, *Women of Ideas — And What Men Have Done to Them, From Aphra Behn to Adrienne Rich*, Routledge Keegan Paul, London, 1983, p. 4.
3. Dorothy Brock, "The Girls' School", in J. Dover Wilson (ed.), *The Schools of England — A Study in Renaissance*, Sidgwick and Jackson Ltd, London, 1928, p. 155.
4. Caesare Lombroso, *The Female Offender*, T. Fisher Unwin, London, 1895; for a critique of this view and others equally offensive and unhelpful, see S. K. Mukherjee and Jocelynne A. Scutt, *Women and Crime*, George Allen and Unwin, Sydney, 1981.
5. See Spender, *Women of Ideas*, op. cit. (note 2).
6. ibid.
7. T. Wilson, *Arte of Rhetorique*, 1560 edn; reprinted Oxford University Press, England, 1909, p. 189.
8. J. Kirby, *A New English Grammar*, Menston, England, 1746, p. 117.
9. W. Ward, *An Essay on Grammar*, Menston, England, 1765, pp. 459-60.
10. Farley Kelly, "Feminism and the Family — Brettena Smyth", in Eric Fry (ed.), *Rebels and Radicals*, George Allen and Unwin, Sydney, 1983, p. 136.
11. Louise Lawson, "The Bonnet", *The Dawn* (No. 3), 1 July 1891; quoted Brian Matthews, "Dawn Crusade — Louise Lawson" in Fry, *Rebels and Radicals*, op. cit. p. 156.
12. See Susan Magarey, "Radical Women — Catherine Spence", in Fry, op. cit., p. 121.
13. That the media should find it necessary to promote Elizabeth Reid as a "first" at all serves to deny her own strengths as an

individual who was chosen to take on a difficult role, and to fill it in a strong, capable, and imaginative way. She had far more to offer than a momentary flash as the first woman "X". It also serves to deny the women's advisers to government and politicians at other times, in other roles. Jessie Street, although not holding an identical position as that of Prime Minister's Adviser on Women's Affairs, was one of a number of women (although that number is not large) who advised in various capacities.

14. See Spender, *Women of Ideas*, op. cit. (note 1).
15. Annmarie Turnbull, "'So Extremely Like Parliament': The Work of the Women Members of the London School Board, 1870-1904", in London Feminist History Group (eds), *Men's Power, Women's Resistance — The Sexual Dynamics of History*, Pluto Press, London, 1983, pp. 125-6.
16. Joan Mills, "What Women Say About Themselves", in Leta W. Clark (ed.), *Women, Women, Women — Quips, Quotes, and Commentary*, Drake, New York, 1977.
17. Elizabeth Cady Stanton, quoted in Carol McPhee and Ann FitzGerald (compilers), *Feminist Quotations — Voices of Rebels, Reformers and Visionaries*, Thomas Y. Crowell, New York, 1979.

Chapter six **Epilogue**

1. See Dale Spender, *Women of Ideas — and What Men Have Done to Them, From Aphra Behn to Adrienne Rich*, Routledge Keegan Paul, London, 1983; Dale Spender, *There's Always Been a Women's Movement this Century*, Pandora Press, London, 1983. In the post-1975 period there was a strong implication, often fostered by the media, that "the women's movement was 'dead' ". In 1978 the first "Women and Labour Conference" organised by Sue Bellamy and others at Macquarie University, when over two thousand women from all age groups and backgrounds met to discuss feminist research and practice, showed the falsity of the claim. Since 1978, amongst many other developments the Women and Labour Conferences have been held at two yearly intervals in Melbourne, Adelaide and Brisbane. Women's liberation and feminist action, research, writing, conferences and ovulars have taken many varying paths and topics.
2. Quoted Carol McPhee and Ann FitzGerald (compilers), *Feminist Quotations — Voices of Rebels, Reformers and Visionaries*, Thomas Y. Crowell, New York, 1979.
3. ibid.

Index

Herbert, Sir Sydney, 140
history, women's 139–41, 147–52

identity, 118
inequality *see* discrimination; equality
infanticide, 111
influences, 25, 26, 33, 34, 35, 149, 150–3,
  155–6, 158–9, 166–7
  see also family; fathers; friends; mothers;
    role models
Ingvarson, Carolyn and Jones, Anne, 11, 21
International Women's Year, 167
In the Marriage of Cartwright, 123
In the Marriage of N. and N., 122
In the Marriage of Spry and Spry, 122–3
intuition, 142
in-vitro fertilisation, 105

journalism and writing, 2, 3, 32, 33, 35–6,
  95, 97, 142–3, 149, 154, 156–7

Kelly, Farley, 145–6
Kitson, Mary Cecil, 41

Labor Party *see* ALP
language, 143–5
"latch key children", 117
law profession, 3, 8, 55, 63, 67–8, 69, 70,
  135
  obstacles to entry, 8, 38–9, 40–1
  see also legislation
Lawson, Louisa, 146–7
Lazarre, Jane, 104
Lebowitz, Fran, 149, 155–6
Legal Practitioners Act, 39, 40–1
legislation, 39–42, 52, 57, 69, 70, 93
  anti-discrimination, 16, 44, 52, 69
  and child custody, 109–10
  divorce, 79–84
  and marriage, 90–2
lesbianism, 27, 31, 33, 91, 92, 140, 165
  and children, 121–4
Lombroso, Caesare, 141–2

Macaulay, Catherine, 145
MacIntyre, 116
Mackay, Lee, 125
MacKellar, Michael, 113
maintenance, 80–1, 120–1
"man", 143–4
Manning, William, 7
marriage, 28–9, 34–5, 61, 65–6, 71–93, 166,
  168–9
  attitudes to, 81–3, 87, 95–6, 101–2, 114,
    129, 134
  as a career, 72, 83
  and contracts, 90–1
  de facto, 66, 87, 88–9, 90–1, 92, 96, 129
  and education, 83
  and equality, 89–91, 92, 95, 101–3
  and independence, 95
  law, 72–5, 76–9, 83, 90–2
  pressure for, 64, 65, 83, 91, 102
  and property, 66, 72–5, 76–8, 79–81, 82
  purpose of, 104–5, 114

and women's rights, 84–9
  see also divorce
married women, treatment of, 61, 84, 85–6,
  95–6
Married Women's Property Acts, 42, 79
masculine mind, 142
maternal deprivation, 117–18
maternal instinct, 110–14, 115
Matrimonial Causes Act 1959, 80–1
Mead, Margaret, 25, 33, 149
mechanic, 45, 58–62
media, 156–7, 160, 162
Medical Practitioners Acts, 39, 40, 41
medicine, 8, 41
  obstacles to entry, 38–9
middle age, 66, 115, 118
middle class, 2, 66, 154
Mills, Joan, 138, 152
Mitchell, Juliet, 37
money, 37, 38, 46–51, 84, 85–6, 89, 159
Morris, Meaghan, 149, 156
motherhood, 107, 110–12, 113, 115, 118,
  119, 124, 157
  importance of, 104–6, 107, 115, 117
  redefining, 124–6
  and rights, 108–10, 117
mothers, influence of, 2, 25–6, 28, 29, 64–5,
  94–5, 128, 132–3, 154, 163, 164–5, 166,
  167
Murray, Elizabeth, 145

National Wage Case, 47, 53
networking, 21, 151–2, 156
  see also support
Nightingale, Florence, 140
Nin, Anais, 166
Norris, Sam, 77–8
Norton, Lady Caroline, 77–8, 109–10
nuclear family, 124, 166
  changing, 125
nursing, 140

Ogden, Ex parte, 42
O'Shane, Pat, 70
Other Choices for Becoming a Woman, 25

Pankhurst, Emily, 26, 149
patriarchy, 105, 107, 124
pay, equal, 37, 38, 46–51, 89
peace movement, 62, 69, 99, 158–9, 171
peer group, 1, 32, 165
personal space, 89–90
persons, women are not, 39–42, 76–7
Pogrebin, Letty Cottin, 5
Poole, Millicent, 18
Porter, Paige, 6
"post-feminist generation", 160
poverty, 63
power, 15, 16
  see also control; dominance
press shops, 53, 54
professions, 55, 69, 135, 147
  see also law profession; medicine
property ownership, 72–93 *passim*